A Visitor's Guide to
CORNWALL
and the
ISLES OF SCILLY

ST AUSTELL

Visitor's Guide Series

This series of guide books gives, in each volume, the details and facts needed to make the most of a holiday in one of the tourist areas of Britain and Europe. Not only does the text describe the countryside, villages, and towns of each region, but there is also valuable information on where to go and what there is to see. Each book includes, where appropriate, stately homes, gardens and museums to visit, nature trails, archaeological sites, sporting events, steam railways, cycling, walking, sailing, fishing, country parks, useful addresses — everything to make your visit more worthwhile.

Other titles already published or planned include:
The Lake District (Revised Edition)
The Peak District
The Chilterns
The Cotswolds
North Wales
The Yorkshire Dales
Devon
Somerset and Dorset
The Scottish Borders and Edinburgh
Dordogne (France)
Guernsey, Alderney and Sark

A Visitor's Guide To
CORNWALL
AND THE
ISLES OF SCILLY

Rita Tregellas Pope

MOORLAND PUBLISHING

British Library Cataloguing
in Publication Data

Pope, Rita
  A visitor's guide to Cornwall and the
  Isles of Scilly
  1. Cornwall (England) — Description
  and travel
  — Guide-books   2. Isles of Scilly
  Description and travel — Guide-books
  I. Title
  914.23'7'04857   DA670.2

The colour illustrations were provided by:
G. Irving (Cothele, Fowey, windsurfing,
St Austell, Polperro, Veryan); Jean A.
Paton (Trewavas Head, Nanjizal, St
Mawes); R.T. Pope (Cheesewring); L.
Porter (China clay);J.A. Robey (Wheal
Martyn, Penzance); P. Vage (St Michael's
Mount).
  The black-and-white illustrations were
provided by: R.H. Bird pp 13, 29, 49, 64,
65, 85; F.E. Gibson pp 69, 72, 73, 74, 75;
D. Hills (courtesy L. Truran) pp 40, 53,
54; R.T. Pope pp 23, 25, 67, 119; L. Porter
p 60; all other photographs were taken by
R.S. Pope. V.S. Paton drew the maps.
  Both author and publisher would like
to acknowledge the assistance given by the
above in providing illustrations.

Printed in the UK by
Butler and Tanner Ltd, Frome
for the publishers
Moorland Publishing Co Ltd,
9-11 Station Street, Ashbourne,
Derbyshire, DE6 1DE England.

Contents

Preface

Cornwall is a land of lovely beaches, magnificent cliffs and fascinating winding lanes. All are beautiful, but they can be dangerous. For your own safety, please observe the warnings displayed by lifeguards and coastguards, and drive carefully along the lanes. Some have passing places, but not all; so be ready to reverse — sometimes quite a distance.

These narrow roads began as tracks made by farm animals, and offer a special relaxation for those who are willing to travel slowly, occasionally perhaps even making time to 'Stand and Stare'. Our wish is that you will return home relaxed, happy, and, above all — safe.

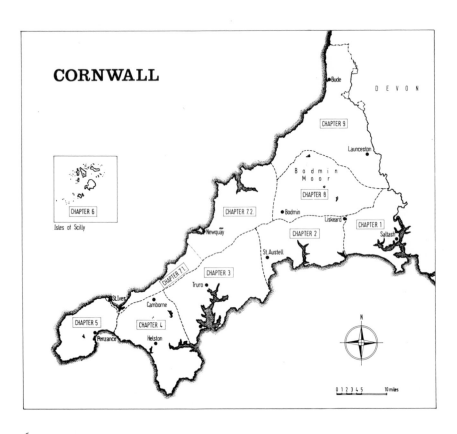

CORNWALL

Introduction

The land of King Arthur — the Cornish Riviera — the Delectable Duchy — call it what you will. Few places have as many facets as Cornwall but this is because the land west of the Tamar is not just a holiday region; it is much more. It is a nation in its own right. Look carefully and you will find what you seek, whether it be tales of the past, pleasures of the present, or even glimpses into the future.

Until the middle of the last century, few people visited Cornwall. Roads were dangerous, and sea travel largely restricted to packet ships and merchantmen. But this state of affairs ended abruptly in 1859, when Brunel's great railway bridge carried the first train over the Tamar into Cornwall. That historic event was the 'Open Sesame' for visitors. At first they came in a thin trickle, but soon others realised the attraction of the land beyond England, and the era of the holidaymaker had begun.

There are, however, those who say that they can find nothing to do in Cornwall. Perhaps they have not troubled to look. The Cornish motto of ONE AND ALL has many interpretations, and the appropriate choice for this guide is ONE place and something for ALL. S.P.B. Mais said that Cornwall has a 'diversity of riches', and as those same treasures have shaped its development, a brief look at the past will show how their mosaic influences have formed the Duchy of today.

With the sea on three sides and the Tamar making the fourth boundary, Cornwall has always been almost an island. So when wandering tribes from Europe arrived, they were able to enjoy a life of comparative peace — scarcely disturbed by the hordes who ravaged the rest of the mainland. That is why, with only wind and weather to affect them, so many Neolithic and Bronze Age monoliths and barrows remain.

The richness of Cornwall's mineral deposits was not exploited until about 350 BC, when Iron Age tribes from Europe came in search of tin. The people of this fair-haired, blue-eyed, race were tall and finely built, probably the originals of the 'giants' in Cornish folklore. They brought their knowledge of tin production with them as well as their culture and a completely new social structure. Evidence of this important occupation is still to be seen in hill forts, cliff castles and the 'trevs' or settlements. The area of West Penwith, beyond Penzance, also retains low dry stone walls and unique small fields — the latter have been cultivated continuously since Iron Age times.

The Tre-, Pol- and Pen- prefixes to family and place names, so typical of Cornwall, also stem from the Iron Age period. For those tribes introduced the Indo-European Celtic language which, in Cornwall, is the Brythonic branch. Although it died out as the universally spoken tongue more than two centuries ago, it is now enjoying a revival.

The much-maligned Druids were Celtic priests who, far from being mere growers of mistletoe, lovers of apples and makers of bonfires, were, in fact, the most highly respected scholars of their day. Men travelled across Europe to learn from them, early Greece was indebted to them and even the great Cicero paid tribute to their knowledge. People who laugh at them have only heard about their more sensational customs, and would doubtless be surprised to know that the Druids were among the first of the so-called pagans to proclaim a doctrine of immortality.

Visitors interested in Roman remains will find few here. The Romans did not settle in Cornwall but their merchants came here for tin, so the Romano-Cornish association was mainly through trade.

The next arrivals were of great importance, for they led the Cornish people away from Druidism to Christianity. These were holy men and women from Wales and Ireland who established their 'cells' near water — rivers, wells or springs, many of which, previously objects of pagan worship, then became shrines and places of pilgrimage. Today about a hundred holy wells still exist, most of them pleasant places to visit; others are looked upon as serving a special purpose — turning the affections of a loved one in the right direction, for example! Cornish churches (many near wells or water) are dedicated to these 'saints' and have names not seen in other English counties, such as St Gluvias, St Probus and St Petrock.

For centuries, Cornwall was entirely Celtic, but once the Anglo-Saxons had overcome England they turned to the west for further conquests. There they met fierce resistance from Cornish chiefs or kings. One was Arthur, a Celtic ruler, born in the late fifth century AD, who led the last great Celtic battle against the Anglo-Saxons. The legends that grew up after his death and the mediaeval romances associated with his name, have so obscured the historical figure that it is now almost impossible to discover the truth about him. By the end of the seventh century the Anglo-Saxons had conquered Devon, but it was not till after AD926 that King Athelstan finally overcame the Cornish. A few Anglo-Saxons settled in Cornwall, mostly along the eastern border. Some ventured further, the evidence for which is the scatter of non-Cornish place names found elsewhere — Wicca at Zennor being a good example.

The Norman Conquest, however, brought many changes. King William's custom of rewarding his barons with large estates held good in Cornwall — even to Land's End. The Domesday Book must have looked impressive with its accounts of groups of manors belonging to various Norman overlords. But many of the so-called manors were little more than small farmsteads or 'trevs', run by perhaps two people as they had been since Celtic times. In many cases, these homesteads are still farmed today, and are to be found almost hidden in a maze of narrow winding lanes. Here Cornwall has scarcely altered for centuries, and those who wish to walk back in time need simply to take the latest OS map and explore the narrow lanes of a remote parish. These lead to the very heart of Cornwall.

The castles the Normans built for defence — Launceston, Restormel and Trematon — served also to restore the sense of security that the Cornish had lost since the Saxon conflicts. By the mid-twelfth century, Cornwall was Europe's largest supplier of tin, and Stannary towns grew up at places where tin was tested. Royal charters for markets and fairs also encouraged trade while the building of numerous collegiate and other churches resulted in a more settled way of life. By 1337,

Cornwall was therefore a fitting Duchy for King Edward III to bestow on his heir, the Black Prince.

In the Middle Ages, however, there was less need for defensive castles; so the landowners built manors with a degree of fortification, a good example being Cotehele, overlooking the Tamar, one of Cornwall's most beautiful great houses.

At sea, as on land, Cornwall prospered. Her sailors and fishermen gained renown at home and abroad. Perhaps one of her proudest occasions was when Fowey sent forty-seven ships (nearly twice the number mustered by the City of London) to help King Edward III besiege Calais in 1347.

But sad times lay ahead. When the Reformation came, Cornwall's beautiful churches were stripped, and most of her collegiate establishments were closed. Men no longer crossed Europe to study at Penryn's famous Glasney College — what might have been Cornwall's university is now only a few stones in and around the town. The final blow, however, came when Bibles were printed in English — a language Cornishmen did not want to understand, and certainly could not read. In an effort to preserve their culture, their way of life and their long heritage, the people rebelled. Many lost their lives in the 1549 Prayer Book Rebellion, but in vain. From then on, the language began to disappear. There is a saying among the Cornish: *An lavar goth, yu lavar gwyr*. It means: 'He who loses his tongue [his language] shall lose his land.' And it came true, for, as the language died, so did the customs and the life of the nation. Today, Cornwall's true identity is to be found only among the shadows of the past.

Prosperity returned briefly, however, in the eighteenth and nineteenth centuries, when underground mining came into its own. The inventions of great Cornish engineers like Richard Trevithick, Michael Loam and Goldsworthy Gurney, enabled shafts to be sunk deep into the ground and even under the sea bed and the increasing number of engine houses and stacks transformed much of the landscape. Fortunes were made and lost again, when copper prices fell and cheap surface tin was imported from Malaya. Once again Cornwall faced disaster. This time, miners emigrated to look for work. Many settled in Canada, Australia, South Africa, Tasmania and the United States; whole families died out and Cornwall's glory faded again.

But there is much of the phoenix in this land. Its story has been mainly influenced by its landscape and by its rocks. Granite has been the source of shelter in life and protection in death; tin and copper and, more recently, china clay, have provided wealth and employment.

1 Around Saltash

Saltash lies on the Cornish side of the River Tamar, and visitors generally arrive either by the A38 or train via Plymouth. The name is a reminder of days when Romans, Anglo-Saxons and Normans used this 'passage' or 'esse', the meeting place of salt and fresh water. King John granted it borough status, and in 1270 the lords of nearby Trematon Castle owned the ferry. Soon the town held jurisdiction over the tidal reaches of both the Tamar and the Lynher, extending their claims on oysterage and anchorage until they controlled all tolls as far as the Calstock salmon weirs.

By 1752, traders and fishermen rebelled against the Saltash monopoly and refused to pay their tolls. The burgesses applied to Parliament for

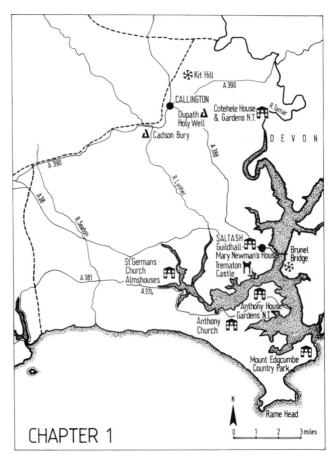

CHAPTER 1

confirmation of rights, but were strongly opposed by James Tillie of Pentillie Castle. As he owned Halton Quay, a little way up river, and several trading vessels, he was considerably affected. He gained support from the Governor of Plymouth and eventually won the law suit brought against him. Finally, he instructed the ships' masters to pay only 1s, an act which made them free for ever 'from all encroachments of the unjust and iniquitous Saltashers.'

The town did not send members to Parliament after 1832 and consequently declined in political importance. It kept its reputation as a great 'nursery' for sailors, however, and even more celebrated were its fisherwomen, who frequently beat all comers in four-oared gig races at various regattas.

When Isambard Brunel built his great bridge across the Tamar in 1859, it brought the first holiday makers to Cornwall and a temporary, slight,

Brunel's bridge

Places of Interest at Saltash

Brunel's Royal Albert Bridge
Railway bridge from Plymouth to Saltash
The last engineering achievement of Isambard Kingdom Brunel, begun in 1857, was opened by Prince Albert on 6 May 1859.

The Guildhall
Fore Street
This was formerly a Market House, but the Town Hall was added in the eighteenth century. By 1890 it became the Guildhall.

Mary Newman's House
Culver Street
This little low Tudor house was the birthplace of Sir Francis Drake's first wife.

---

revival to Saltash. When the Admiralty bought the oyster rights in 1901, the town's long maritime history ended. Recently, however, it has found a new identity as a prosperous, friendly shopping centre, remembering its past in certain buildings.

On the corner of Fore Street and Station Road is the present fine Guildhall. Over the centuries it has been market hall and town hall, now resplendent both inside and out, and worthy of its name. The upstairs assembly hall is used for every kind of meeting from politics to popular markets as well as the Mayor-choosing ceremony. (The mayoral insignia has a special local interest in that it includes three silver oars with maceheads.) Closely associated with it is the church of St Nicholas and St Faith. This was a chapel of ease until 1881; the building dates from about 1225, although the tower is earlier and the clock (about 1720) is a rarity for Cornwall.

Much of Saltash's history has been linked with the villages along the banks of the Tamar. On the A388 Callington road lies Carkeel, where an industrial estate offers work in Cornwall for local people who do not want to go to Plymouth. A right-hand turn in the centre of the village — so narrow that it can easily be missed — leads to tree-lined lanes, winding round to Botus Fleming, set high above the Tamar. A memorial to the Symons family is in the church — an unusual wooden reredos which shows the agricultural nature of the area, with its vines, corn and various fruits. There is also a memorial brass to one of Cornwall's great engineers, Michael Loam, inventor of the 'man engine' which helped miners to ascend and descend the deep mine shafts, and so saved many lives. Born in West Cornwall, he died in 1871 at Moditonham House, where only twelve years before, the Prince of Orange had surrendered Pendennis and Plymouth Castles. During World War II, Moditonham suffered considerable bomb damage, but the National Trust now maintains the little that is left.

Lanes to Cargreen are warm with meadow-sweet and bright with purple vetch in summer. Linger beside the quiet quay — a pleasant place to watch the small craft. Walkers may prefer to take the bypass to Landulph church.

A handful of cottages hug Cargreen Quay. The village has a lively yacht club, but it is hard to realise that this was once Cornwall's Covent Garden. Market gardeners from all over the valley brought their produce here to be ferried across to Devon. Now only sailing boats and birds make the crossing — a walk beside the river at low tide reveals the Tamar at its loveliest; it is an area beloved of bird-watchers and naturalists.

Motorists climb gently away from

Places of Interest North of Saltash

Cotehele
(National Trust)
St Dominick, beside the Tamar
A romantic medieval house of grey granite, built 1485-1627. One of the best preserved examples of a squire's house, for centuries home of the Edgcumbes. Beautifully furnished with original tapestries, needlework and armour.

Kit Hill
2 miles NE of Callington beside the A390
An outlying eminence of granite, the summit of Hingston Down where King Egbert defeated the Britons and Danes in AD 835.

Dupath Holy Well
1m from Callington between A388 and A390
This is the largest well building in Cornwall.

Cargreen, past Coombe Lane, where wool was collected from local farmers en route to a mill at Liskeard. The turning to the right after the church climbs high above the valley again, and ferny lanes give way to open views. Pentillie Castle, superbly sited to overlook a wooded sweep of the river, may be seen on the right. It was first built in 1689 by James Pentillie, a steward to the Coryton family of Cornwall's Newton Ferrers. When Pentillie's greatniece married a Coryton in 1810, Wilkins, who designed London's National Gallery, planned the alterations. Further work, carried out between 1965 and 1970 has made the castle almost the same as the original. Granite pillars from Kit Hill make the front look impressive, while a statue of James Pentillie in the centre of the courtyard seems to register approval.

Calstock, in the Tamar Valley

Beyond this, narrow lanes climb then dip into the strangely-named Mount Ararat woods, before dropping steeply to the peace of Halton Quay. The Pentillie fleet ferried Hingston Down granite from here to Devon in the eighteenth century and cargoes of local fruit and flowers downriver. Since the quay closed in 1926, birdlovers and fishermen have taken over and the chapel of St Dominick beside the water is once again a place of quiet.

From here, even narrower lanes lead up past Chapel Farm to the village of St Dominick where there is the one remaining cherry orchard of the many which used to supply markets all over the country.

In the next valley lie the mill and riverside buildings of Cothele — the manor on the hill above overlooking the Tamar. This romantic Tudor mansion was formerly the home of the Edgcumbes; built between 1485 and 1627, it contains all the original Tudor furnishings. The valley garden has a well-restored dovecote, and on the walk through the woods to the quay is the Edgcumbe chapel, built by Sir Richard as a thankoffering for his survival after declaring against the Crown in 1403.

Cothele is not a place to rush away from. The whole area is ideal for a day's pleasure with walks, bird-watching, and sometimes salmon-fishing to watch. Picnic where you will, explore house and riverside buildings, and marvel at the craftsmanship of *Shamrock*, the last surviving stone-carrying Tamar barge.

For walkers and birdwatchers, there is a river footpath to Calstock, but motorists have to follow more narrow ferny lanes to this attractive village — another quiet place but once a busy shipyard. The handsome railway viaduct brought trains to the village but destruction to its shipping. Today, pleasure boats make pleasant pictures as they sail past the place where James Goss built the *Garlandstone,* Britain's last ketch. Most river and fishing ports have always had regattas, but Calstock's — as famous as those of Saltash — has recently been revived.

The road out of Calstock under the railway bridge is signposted Tavistock, but along the road look for a sign to Calcraft Products. Here suits of armour are made to measure and antique-style pistols fashioned to individual designs.

Gunnislake village clings to an even steeper slope than Saltash; the road to New Bridge calls for low gear and good brakes. Before stagecoaches demanded roads and not muddy byways, the approaching paths to the river went straight down the cliff side — a daunting gradient even on horseback. Piers Edgcumbe of Cothele built this Tamar bridge in 1520 and in 1644 Sir Richard Grenville did his utmost to defend it against the Roundheads. It was then the chief pass into Cornwall, but Sir Richard's efforts were unfortunately in vain.

At this point, the Tamar 'tastes the tide' and just as its maritime trading interests are now ceasing, it is appropriate to turn inland again. The A390 Callington road runs at the foot of Kit Hill, but one should turn off on the B3257 for the lane to the top. The Duchy of Cornwall preserved the 85ft stack at the summit — a mining monument to the workers who won tin over the centuries and who, with Devon men, held their Stannary Parliaments there. On a clear day the views extend to Dartmoor's Hessary Tor 12 miles (20km) away, the Eddystone Lighthouse 23 miles (37km) and west to Bodmin

Moor and Roughtor 15 miles (24km). There are old mine workings among the heather, and in good weather, a whole day may be enjoyed here.

Before entering Callington, is a minor road on the left signposted to St Mellion. A short way down, another lane leads to Dupath Well, a handsomely covered spring, the largest of its kind in Cornwall.

Quiet Callington was once the centre of a thriving wool industry and, before that, some believe it to have been the site of King Arthur's palace of Killiwic. By the main car park is Celliwic Crafts, where courses on pottery, iron work and spinning are available, while the shop gallery displays local paintings and garments knitted from locally bred sheep: the farmer's wife carries out the whole process.

Just out of the town is a little lane beside the church, Tillie Street, now reduced to one cottage. This was the birthplace of John Knill, St Ives' well-known and controversial mayor.

The Liskeard A390 road narrows immediately outside the town into country lanes which dip to picturesque Newbridge. The earliest mention of a bridge here was in 1478. This is a typical Cornish 'trev' where the settlement was once high above on Cadson Bury, a prehistoric fort now National Trust property. It is worth stopping to walk up and enjoy the views down the Lynher valley.

St Ive (Eve) hamlet sits clean and fresh beside the busy road. The church, a Knights Templar's foundation, was built in 1180. A narrow lane opposite the slate-hung Butcher's Arms leads down to Quethiock (Gwithick). This compact village seems to surround its church protectively, perhaps because of the fine large Kyngdon brass. Roger and his wife had sixteen children and they are all shown quite clearly by the craftsman who worked it in 1471. (The key is at Well Cottage if the church is locked.) This remote parish of twisting lanes and secluded farmhouses leads a busy life of its own — one of the highlights being the Agricultural Show held in mid-July. The standards are high, and everyone is made welcome.

From here to St Mellion, the lanes dip and twist in almost impossible configurations, but in high summer they are cool and delightful. It matters little whether you find the clapper bridge at Bramble Wood, or take the way to Pillatonmill and climb out of the deep valley from there, for both roads are little used. Mid-July is the time to visit St Mellion and its Cherry-Pie Feast. Squire Coryton of Pentillie originated this, inviting local schoolchildren to a cherry-pie and cream tea on the lawn of the castle. Swings were set up in the 200-year-old lime trees bordering the mile-long drive from the road, and everyone looked forward to this annual event. The Rev and Mrs Watts revived a local tradition in 1975 and adapted it as a replacement for their Summer Garden Party. Sometimes local cherries are used for the pies, but they are not always as readily available as they were in Squire Coryton's time.

The countryside south of Saltash has attractions quite different from those of the Tamarside villages. A glance at the map shows that this area can be explored in two parts, but only by returning along the same road.

The road from Saltash dips to Forder from its mother church, St Stephen's. Here, nearly two miles from the town centre, is fine countryside with Trematon Castle outlined on the distant hill. In the valley, mill buildings and a cluster of old Tudor cottages huddle together, watching the traffic climb sharply to the lodge gates of Trematon Castle. Those who prefer may walk the lower way and watch the trains lumbering slowly round from Saltash after carefully negotiating Brunel's bridge — the engineering triumph of the time. Today, the high granite shafts and unusual tubular arches give it a strange look, but the result has always been the same — efficiency combined with safety, the first considerations for a railway bridge.

Train passengers, walkers and motorists, all enjoy their brief glimpse of Trematon Castle. Possibly the most extensive in Cornwall, it has a well-preserved keep, 'one of the most beautiful examples of the Norman period'. It passed into Duchy hands in the fourteenth century, and figured in a particularly distressing incident which occurred during the Prayer Book Rebellion, when Sir Richard and Lady Grenville were captured by treachery.

Beyond the castle, as the road dips to the riverside chapel, a stumpy wayside cross shows the important part once played by this out-of-the-way route.

Ince Castle, beside the Lynher, is another private residence. Built by the Killigrews in the sixteenth century, it resembles a French chateau. It is alleged that at one time the Killigrew owner kept four wives, and allocated a tower to each of them — a tale as picturesque as the castle itself.

There is no way for motorists to cross the Lynher River, but the short distance along the A38 to Tideford (or Tiddyford) is not unpleasant. This roadside village takes its name from the River Tiddy, quietly flowing down through farm and wood until it meets the salt water here.

The riverside walk is a pleasant way to reach the village of St Germans. Motorists, however, can turn left on to

Places of Interest South of Saltash

Trematon Castle
1 mile SW of Saltash
One of a group of Norman fortresses, built either by Earl Mortain or the Valletorts. Now privately owned.

St Germans
The church was the seat of the Cornish bishopric from the close of the tenth to the early eleventh century. Its great feature is the Norman west door.
The Almshouses, built by Sir William Moyle in 1538, were restored in 1967.

Antony House (National Trust)
About 15 miles from Saltash
A Carew-Pole property since the fifteenth century, this house was built in the early eighteenth century. The Bath House can be seen on application to the Secretary.
Extensive grounds slope to the River Lynher.

Antony Church
Rededicated in 1259, this church is mainly remarkable for its spectacular early brass (1420) to Lady Margery Arundell.

Mount Edgcumbe House
Entrance at Cremyll Ferry
Originally built in 1547-54 for Sir Richard Edgcumbe, but destroyed in 1941 blitz. Rebuilt 1960. Home of the present earl, and open in summer on Monday and Tuesday afternoons.

Mount Edgcumbe Country Park
Eight hundred acres of parkland on magnificent coastline are open all the year. No charge.

Rame Head
Stretching in to sea beyond Rame church (St German) with expansive views east and west.

the B3249. Behind the Information Centre and under the arch lies Heskyn Mill Restaurant, once used for corn and flax — now a pleasant place for a meal. Along the lane is Cutcrew, the oldest working saw mill in the Tiddy Valley and one of the few left in Cornwall. The waterwheel is being restored and there are plans to use it for special joinery, including restoring antique furniture. This interesting mill complex has a craft gallery and tea rooms.

The village of St Germans, three miles along the B3249, a picturesque composition of cottages and flower-filled gardens, was once a rotten borough sending two MPs to Westminster. At the slope into the village, notice Sir William Moyle's Almshouses. Built in 1538, they were skilfully reconditioned in 1967 at the instigation of the National Association of Almshouses.

St Germans, Cornwall's ancient cathedral, stands among trees away from the traffic. This building, consecrated in 1261, had been an Augustinian priory before that. The great west door, Cornwall's finest, is a powerful example of Norman architecture, made of elvan stone from Tartan Down near Landrake; the church's spacious and lofty interior contains numerous interesting features. Since 1974 the diocese of Truro has had a bishop suffragan of St Germans.

Close by, the Tudor gateway, housing an antique shop, leads to Port Eliot where the Eliot family has lived for four hundred years. It is probably Cornwall's largest private house, bought by Sir Thomas Elyot when Cardinal Wolsey was selling monastery lands. This member of the family was not only an astute business man, but a skilled ambassador and the first person to compile an English dictionary. Perhaps

St Germans Church

the best known member of the family, however, was Sir John, an MP and a Vice-Admiral of Devon. His great interest in maritime affairs brought him to the Tower and an untimely death, for opposing the king's Bills of Tonnage and Poundage, which he considered would impose too great a strain on the mercantile community. In 1762, Sir Humphrey Repton redesigned the gardens and Sir John Soane made certain architectural alterations, including the addition of a splendid round room, some forty feet in diameter. The present Lord Eliot administers all six thousand acres and sells produce from the walled garden in the Bothy Shop. During July's last weekend an Elephant Fayre is held in the grounds. The name of this four-day spectacle of music, theatre, film, dance and craft comes, not from its size, but from the animal whose head appears on the family crest.

The view up river through the thirteen arches of the railway viaduct seen from St Germans' Quay is a fine sight on a sunny day. Once through Polbathic, a whole stretch of woodland walks and picnic areas awaits those who explore the paths to Sheviock and Antony, in the peninsula which has been called a miniature kingdom. Antony House was built in the early eighteenth century and is the most distinguished classic house in Cornwall. Though now owned by the National Trust it is still the home of the Carew-Poles. Two hundred and fifty acres of grounds slope gently to the Lynher — the walks here and in the gardens are not to be missed in summer. An interesting Bath House ($\frac{1}{2}$ mile from house) open by appointment only, was built in 1784 and has recently been repaired. Antony church should not be missed either — the early brass of Lady Margery Arundell (1420) is the most spectacular in the whole of Cornwall.

Torpoint seems a mere mass of uninteresting buildings after the great house of Antony, but it has its own features for the visitor. In 1691, William of Orange's order for the construction of Cattewater naval dockyard in Plymouth was followed by such activity that Torpoint came into existence. According to Daniel Defoe, not only did the workmen need homes, but the operation needed 'yards, dry docks, launches, and conveniences of all kinds, for building and repairing of ships!' Little is left of that undertaking now, although some of the old quays with their slate wharves still remain near the ferry. In 1793, the ferryman at this important crossing was obliged to keep three boats for pedestrians and one for horses, charging all passengers a penny for the return journey. Today, pedestrians travel free from Torpoint, while wheeled vehicles have to pay a small charge.

Antony House

The road inland to Millbrook passes the naval establishment of HMS Raleigh, before cutting sharply across to St John. This is a place of contrast, a mediaeval cluster of narrow lanes in a fold of hills and matching cottages. At low tide, the best way is by the road across the ford at the head of St John's Lake. Birdwatchers and walkers will be tempted to linger here.

Further on is the little town of Millbrook. The roads are narrow and winding with Georgian houses jostling against humble but picturesque cottages.

The road to Cremyll goes first through Maker Heights in a steep climb, looking down on Millbrook as a toy town of childish delight. Then from the top of the world the B3247 slides down to quiet Cremyll, a small group of houses at the crossing named the Passage of Crimela in thirteenth-century charters. Here is a place that retains its individuality and its old houses, but the

toll keeps up to date! Watching Drake Island and the shipping in Plymouth Sound keeps Cremyll busy all the year round, and visitors are welcome to park and join the game.

From here is a walk into Mount Edgcumbe Park, eight hundred acres of superb parkland, bordered by ten miles of magnificent coastline. During the summer, there are refreshments in the eighteenth-century orangery of the Italian Gardens, with follies and a handsome conservatory not far away. The house itself is the home of the seventh Earl of Edgcumbe.

Walks from here to Rame Head, (about two and a half miles away) skirt the park and continue through Maker parish, Cawsand and Kingsand. There are distant views of Plymouth Breakwater and across to Heybrook Bay from Penlee Point, before arriving at the headland.

Motorists have to climb again to

Maker Heights before dipping down narrow lanes to Kingsand and Cawsand Bay at the water's edge. Till 1835 this area was not part of Cornwall — Boundary Cottage still exists as a memory marker. Few people know that this was the birthplace of young Burke, the loyal sailor believed to have shot the Frenchman whose bullet killed Lord Nelson. Kingsand is still a sailor's place — the streets twist like an anchor rope in a storm, and the cottages cling to the cliff as seamen to the mast in rough weather. Most drivers miss Halfway House and are soon in and out of Cawsand.

Once away from the villages, the road to Rame seems to continue for ever, giving the strange sensation of driving into the sea. There is a car park beyond the church for those wishing to explore the headland. Near the sea is the ancient chapel of St Michael where hermits once kept lights burning to warn ships of the rocks. In 1488, however, men were paid for this, receiving 4d for 'Keeping of ye bekyng'.

From here to Seaton the road keeps close to the cliff top, as does the coastal path and, in fine weather, the views are superb. Portwrinkle's golf course on the cliffs is almost the only sign of life till Downderry. Beyond is Seaton — a place of sands and summer enjoyment for those who like crowds. A great attraction at Murrayton is the world's first protected breeding colony of Amazon woolly monkeys. They live in a sanctuary, not a zoo.

In the wooded Seaton valley, leading away from the beach caravans, there is a quiet magic for lovers of birds and trees. It is hard to believe that a few miles away traffic still hurries noisily between Liskeard and Saltash.

Landrake village is not far away. This was the birthplace of Robert Jeffrye, Lord Mayor of London in Charles Stuart's time and founder of Shoreditch almshouses, who also remembered to help Landrake's poor.

2 Liskeard to St Austell

Between Saltash and Lostwithiel lies Liskeard, once a prosperous town trading in tin and wool. Minerals from Caradon Hill brought a charter and subsequent wealth in 1240. Stannary privileges followed in 1307, when Liskeard became a coinage town. Later the flourishing wool trade added to its prosperity. The increasing demand for tin in the eighteenth and nineteenth centuries led to the opening of the Liskeard-Looe Canal, which carried ore and stone supplies to the coast for export. Webb's Hotel in the Square was built in 1833 as a coaching inn.

The church of St Martin, the second largest in Cornwall, dates from the mid-thirteenth century. Stuart House in Barras Street is attractively slate-hung, as it must have been when King Charles stayed there in 1644-5. Traces of the old town linger in and around Well Lane and Market Street, where the Guildhall used to be. The Pipe Well, originally late sixteenth century was restored in the early nineteenth.

Industrial archaeologists or those interested in detective work could spend a pleasant time walking along part of the old canal trackway. Footpaths above

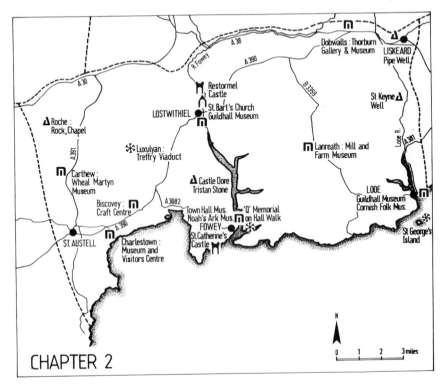

CHAPTER 2

Places of Interest in and around Liskeard

Pipe Well
Well Lane
Originally late sixteenth century.
Restored in early nineteenth century.

St Keyne Well (SX 248602)
About half a mile east of the church
is this famous well. Linked with
legends of wedded bliss — recorded
in 1541.

Cornish Folk Museum
Lower Street, East Looe
In an old fish cellar are items
representing Cornwall's life and
culture.

Old Guildhall Museum
East Looe
Exhibits of Looe's history.

St George's Island
Off Hannafore Point
Private bird sanctuary — visitors
allowed.

Lanreath Mill and Farm Museum
Churchtown, Lanreath
Exhibits of vintage tractors and
implements, granite cider press and
old farmhouse kitchen.

Archibald Thorburn Museum and Gallery
$\frac{1}{2}$ mile north of A38 through
Dobwalls
Unique award-winning collection of
wildlife paintings.

Forest Railroad Park (both under
same management)
Based on the American Railroad —
film shows and models.

---

and below Moorswater are shown on the map.

On the B3254 Looe road is an old industrial mill which houses Liskeard Glass, where craftsmen may be seen shaping their wares. It is open seven days a week and there is a shop.

Beyond Liskeard station is a sign for St Keyne's Well but en route is the Paul Corin Musical Collection. This modern wonder is housed in the family mill deep among lush, narrow lanes beside the Looe River. Here one may listen to instruments ranging in size from the musical box which began it all to a 20ft high Belgian Dance Hall Organ: an amazing collection.

Two winding ways lead the motorist to Cornwall's most famous well, the longer passing through the hill-high village and its church of St Keyne. Set below road level where three lanes meet, this beautifully restored well can easily

be missed. In the past, newly-married couples hurried here after their wedding ceremony, believing that the first to drink the water would rule the household. Robert Southey explained the legend in his poem about it:

Whoso first the water drinks
Thereby the mastery gains.

An idea that would have little appeal for today's liberated brides.

The lane dips steeply past the pleasant St Keyne Well Hotel; turn right at Badham's Farm and then take the right fork. There is no signpost here — the map says it leads through Windsor Wood — but visitors who drive along here in spring may be forgiven for thinking that the direction should be 'To Fairyland'. A grass track in the centre of the road tempts cows from their pasture and motorists must wait while they test the quality of the roadway grass, following as the animals make their leisurely way towards the next gate. Ducks, too, use this wooded valley lane and so peaceful is this place that rejoining the B3254 to Duloe seems like finding an unexpected motorway.

In fact, the village is quiet and attractive, specialising in cottages with country names — it is fun to list them — but having its own memorable past. The church of St Cuby and St Leonard has a well-preserved thirteenth-century tower. One of its rectors was Robert Scott who made his contributions to the Liddell and Scott Greek dictionary during his incumbency. Signposted from the main road is a circle of eight stones, 38ft in diameter, restored in the nineteenth century.

The B3254 joins the A387 at Sandplace and it is worth turning east there for about a mile. Morval House, once owned by the Glynns is a fine building, photogenic, but not open to the public. The church of St Wenna, behind a rhododendron screen, is noteworthy for the fine slate memorial to Walter Coode, his wife and their twelve children; the children are represented allegorically as fruits growing out of vines trailing behind their kneeling parents. Remarkably, the walls seem to lean outwards and a tower pinnacle is crooked.

Looe's golf course is on the other side of Morval, at Widegates. From there the B3253 joins the A387 just outside East Looe. The town had a charter as early as 1237 and much of its past is recorded in the Old Guildhall Museum. Other exhibits of great interest are displayed in the Cornish Museum, Lower Street — once an old fish cellar. There is also, most appropriately, an excellent aquarium at the quay, open for long hours during the season.

Shark fishing, good sailing and swimming can be enjoyed from the little beach by the banjo pier. This is seen at its best from the cliffs of West Looe. The original bridge, built in 1411, was magnificent with thirteen arches and a hermitage chapel, but the present one has only seven arches and was widened in 1960.

Left over the bridge, past the fourteenth-century St Nicholas church is the steep road which leads to Looe Bay. Beyond the rocks lies St George's Island. Once a Celtic monastery, it is now a privately-owned bird sanctuary, an ideal place for a day. It is possible to walk along the coastal path into Polperro from here, but motorists must return to the church and turn left past the 500-year-old inn, The Jolly Sailor.

This narrow, exciting lane to Talland Bay, past the Measured Nautical Mile, cannot be hurried. St Tallan church stands proudly at the top of a precipitous hill leading to the beach — with its strange pink-grey rocks and grey stony sand. Another climb leads to Sclerder Abbey, a gracious, peaceful Carmelite Monastery near the A387.

Much of the coast between Talland Bay and Polperro is National Trust property and fine views offset the rough path. Motorists can enter Polperro by the A387, but the roads were made for horses and it is preferable to park outside the village during the summer — a horsebus ride to the bottom of the hill is a pleasant mode of travel.

Small though the village is, there is a great deal to see — the unspoilt harbour sheltering behind its sturdy wall, the Pilchard Inn where fishermen once had their catch weighed, Couch House where Jonathan Couch was born, and Couch's Great House opposite, now an excellent restaurant with an interior that reads like a history book. But what was Polperro really like before visitors came? The answer is in the Model Village, a replica built by local craftsmen and guaranteed to set the imagination working.

Narrow lanes lead to Lansallos with its fine church high above Lantivet Bay. Unusual are the thirty-four carved bench ends, most of them early sixteenth century. Here, too, are some fine slate-carved memorials and its greatest treasure, Bishop Trelawny's pastoral staff.

To the north, the quiet hamlet of Lanreath is steeped in history — the name recalling a mediaeval monastery and the handsome Court Barton, once the Tudor manor home of the Grylls family. Perhaps the famous 400-year-old Punch Bowl Inn holds the village secrets, for it has been in turn Court House, Coaching Inn and Smugglers' Distribution House. Augustus John stayed there: the unusual inn-sign outside being a reminder of his visit. An added attraction is the fine collection of horse brasses, many, doubtless, from places such as the Lanreath Mill across the road, now operating as a Farm Museum. The past is literally brought to life three times a week by demonstrations of forgecraft, corn dolly work and spinning.

On the way back to Liskeard is the Giant's Hedge, near to which the Lanreath road joins the B3359. This prehistoric earthwork was built by the Devil, according to legend. After about two miles is a right turn for Herodsfoot — walk across country if preferred — and the delights of Forestry Commission nature trails in Deerpark Wood. In this other world there are holiday cabins deep in the valley, overlooking ponds once serving an old gunpowder mill. Sailing, riding and fishing are available for holidaymakers on this self-catering site. To see it at bluebell time is to understand why it won the Civic Trust

Polperro

Award the year after it opened.

Two more award-winning places are signposted at Dobwalls on the A38 to Liskeard: a million pound memorial exhibition to Britain's greatest wildlife artist, Archibald Thorburn, and a miniature American Railroad. Here are among the county's most pleasing attractions, lovingly displayed in a friendly atmosphere; there is enough here for a day's delight.

Eleven miles west, along the A390 from Liskeard, is Lostwithiel. A quiet, welcoming place, a good touring centre where picturesque ruins and an old church are daily reminders of its importance in history from 1100 when the Normans built Restormel Castle. Today the proud shell is well cared for by the Department of the Environment and visitors may picnic there, high above

23

the Looe valley. The town was granted a charter of rights and port status in 1190, and a timber bridge was built to mark a crossing point which had existed since the Bronze Age: it was replaced in the fifteenth century by one of granite, still in use. As by 1272 the increasing tin trade required an assay point, Lostwithiel's Duchy Parliament building incorporated the Stannary Court, the Hall of Exchequer and Exchange as well as the prison. The remains are still to be seen — of particular interest is the cobbled way below a fine stone arch on Fore Street, used by pack animals laden with wool or tin from Bodmin en route for the Stannary Court.

In 1337, Edward III proclaimed his seven-year-old son and heir Duke of Cornwall. When he came of age he was a just overlord, much concerned with his domain of Restormel and Lostwithiel, which he administered wisely and well; the town prospered with tin, tanning and wool trading. In 1644, Roundhead forces overcame the loyal inhabitants and desecrated St Bartholomew's church. It is said, however, that, when Essex's men later surrendered, the people of Lostwithiel took their revenge.

But the parish church, dedicated to the patron saint of tanners more than three hundred years earlier, overcame its indignities. It is still there, three hundred years later, for visitors to admire its unusual features, especially the spire of Breton design added at the same time as the font in the fourteenth century.

The Guildhall Museum in Fore Street is free, as is the town parking. This gives ample opportunity to explore everything — a pottery, antiques, a good bookshop and restaurants. Pay a special visit to The Spinners Web in Queen Street, where the past has been brought to life; there is spinning and weaving for all to see. Weekly classes are also held here and orders taken for handspun wool, cloth and finished garments.

But Lostwithiel is not fossilised in the past; it keeps up to date with galas, fetes and an annual regatta. If your pleasure

Restormel Castle

Lostwithiel Bridge

is fishing, birdwatching, walking or simply enjoying the peace of the country, it is all here. Booklets are available to tell you where the Coulson Park Nature Reserve is and the best way to reach the Duchy Nurseries and an interesting woodland nature trail.

About four miles eastwards along the A390, at West Taphouse, a right-hand turn to Braddock dips and climbs to the church, a delight in spring, but solitary beside woods where historians remember the Civil War and the Battle of Braddock Downs (1643) when Cornishmen put the Parliamentarians to rout and took 1,200 prisoners. Today the Cornish branch of the Sealed Knot re-enact this for their own pleasure and that of many onlookers.

Road and woodland paths, rich in wildlife, pass close to Boconnoc, whose six hundred years of history include a brawling duellist, Thomas 'Diamond' Pitt (cousin to Britain's youngest Prime Minister), and a modern event, when camera crews filmed part of Winston

---

Places of Interest in and around Lostwithiel

Restormel Castle
(Department of the Environment)
1½m north of Lostwithiel
Impressive remains of twelfth-century castle above River Fowey. Has connections with the Black Prince.

St Bartholomew's Church
Lostwithiel
Dedicated to the patron saint of tanners, probably built in twelfth century.

Guildhall Museum
Fore Street, Lostwithiel
Built 1740, this has linenfold panelling, town insignia and copies of the charters.

Graham's *Poldark* series for television. The 'No Thoroughfare' road leads to the church — the key may be had from the nearby estate office. It is small but interesting — more a house chapel, but nevertheless with Royal Arms.

Narrow tree-lined lanes lead to the backwaters of Couch's Mill and Lerryn, picturesque villages beside the Lerryn River. There are wooded paths on both sides, but the one north of Lerryn's sixteenth-century bridge goes to Great Wood and looks seawards along the Fowey. It became the Wild Wood in Kenneth Grahame's *Wind in the Willows.* He discovered it during one of his visits to his friend Sir Arthur Quiller-Couch at Fowey. The path reaches the point jutting into the Fowey and turns upstream to St Winnow, a lovely, lonely churchtown — also filmed for *Poldark.* The building has one of Cornwall's few surviving rood screens, Tudor bench ends and fine windows.

From Lerryn the road climbs steeply to St Veep church before dipping to Penpol. Walkers may follow the river and climb to Haye Farm where National Trust land looks across the River Fowey to Golant. Lanteglos Highway was rightly named as it runs on the spine of this largely unspoilt parish. Before taking the steep road to Bodinnick Ferry for Fowey, there is a detour to Lantivet Bay, where a walk to Pencarrow Head has fine views east to Rame and west to the Lizard.

Polruan is quaint and very old, but has had to give way to Fowey — which now claims the first place. In 1066 it was probably the main centre of trade and population at the estuary mouth, but Fowey had a powerful feudal patron to grant and procure necessary privileges, and this led, over the centuries, to Polruan's decline.

Hall Walk, where the 'Q' memorial stands looking downriver, is National Trust property and covers forty acres of cliff. The paths are best early in the year when they are bright with a variety of spring flowers. Today Bodinnick ferry carries vehicles; it has been important since the fourteenth century, forming part of the south coast route from Cremyll.

On the Fowey side of the river, coasters can be seen loading their cargoes of china clay — a different scene from the days when the Fowey Gallants sailed away to the siege of Calais in forty-seven men-o'-war.

June is a good time to visit Fowey. There is room then to wander at leisure through the narrow streets, which twist and turn till one would think that even a cat might lose its way. Every bend brings the past to life again: the Noah's Ark Museum, in the town's oldest house, contains a fascinating collection of exhibits, the Town Museum displays other treasures, the Ship Hotel remembers its days as the Rashleigh's town house, and even the Fowey Gallants have their name perpetuated by one of the yacht clubs. Fowey seems to offer everything: walks, swimming, sailing, fishing and a wealth of archaeological material close by.

The coastal path from the town leads past St Catherine's Castle — now ruined — once one of a chain of south coast forts built by Henry VIII. Gribbin Head is memorable with its huge red and white day mark, built in 1842, providing an unmistakeable warning for shipping. Menabilly, set in the woods behind Polridmouth Cove, and formerly the home of Daphne du Maurier, was used as a setting for her novel *The King's General.*

Beside the B3269 out of Fowey, is the Longstone or the Tristan Stone. Its sixth century inscription is translated as

'TRISTAN, THE SON OF CONOMORUS' (the name by which King Mark was known). Historians now think that Castle Dore, the earthwork a short way off, was the site of Mark's castle, but facts have not yet verified this, and students of Beroul's *Roman de Tristan* continue to puzzle over it.

At Castle Dore a lane to the right leads to Golant, a quiet, sheltered waterside village with more Tristan associations. In the church of St Sampson, King Mark and Queen Iseult worshipped as it was near the castle and Lantyan, also connected with them. Tristan's duel with Morholt possibly took place there, watched, we are told, by Cornish and Irish on opposite banks, looking like 'holm-gang' (invading Northmen). Is that perhaps how the Holbush Inn on the A390 at St Austell acquired its name?

English China Clay — the giant producer of Cornwall's kaolin, has its headquarters at St Austell in the heart of the 'mountains'. It is a pleasant place with old buildings quietly enjoying the life of a mediaeval village in the

Fowey

Places of Interest in and around Fowey

'Q' Memorial on Hall Walk
Granite monolith facing down River Fowey, beloved by Sir Arthur Quiller-Couch, who lived there 1892-1944.

Noah's Ark Museum
Fore Street
Oldest house in Fowey. Exhibits in rooms such as Victorian Parlour, Marine Cellar, etc.

Town Hall Museum
Trafalgar Square
Town history exhibits. Possibly guild chapel — later prison.

Tristan Stone
Beside B3269 outside town
Monolith with sixth-century inscription. ('Tristan Son of Cunomorus').

Castle Dore
2½m north of Fowey
Possibly site of King Mark's castle — actually a circular earthwork.

St Catherine's Castle
¾m south-west of Fowey towards Gribbin
Remains of Henry VIII's harbour fort.

churchtown, away from the new shopping precinct and rumbling white clay lorries. Modern interests thrive at the Arts Centre and Theatre. The B3273 leads to Pentewan where stone from Duchy quarries was in great demand for rebuilding churches during the fifteenth century. William Cookworthy's discovery of china clay at Carloggas in the eighteenth century brought new life to this little port. A harbour was built and waggons took their new loads down to waiting ships until tin-streaming soil and china-clay slurry caused the silting which killed it as a port. Today caravans rest on dunes beside the once prosperous harbour.

A footpath goes part of the way to Black Head but joins the road where the cliff becomes too sheer for walkers. Views across St Austell Bay to Gribbin Head have a touch of mystery about them for the water shimmers with the constant presence of china clay slurry; the effects are strange and ethereal.

Charles Rashleigh began to develop the port of Charlestown for tin in 1791, and it continued to prosper with the growth of the china clay industry. Then J.T. Treffry of Fowey constructed the port of Par which rivalled both Pentewan and Charlestown, and it is still the main china clay port for smaller vessels, although Charlestown remains active, but increasingly as a holiday place. Its Shipwreck Centre is a wet-weather attraction, and the little beach is a pleasant place for fishing, bathing and sailing. Only half a mile along the cliff path is Carlyon Bay offering added attractions — the Cornish Leisure World and Polkyth Recreation Centre together providing everything from table tennis to opera.

Beside the A3082, a stadium for stock car racing caters for a different sport — how would Ralph Allen enjoy it? He was born in a cottage only a few yards along the road towards St Blazey — a small plaque on the wall marks the place. Not many visitors to Cornwall realise that well over a hundred years before Rowland Hill invented the Penny Post, Allen had devised the first real postal system in the country.

There is little of architectural interest in this area, but up the hill past Allen's birthplace is the Mid-Cornwall Craft Centre and Galleries. First class goods for sale are well displayed and it is also possible to take part in art and craft courses.

At the top of the hill is the Four Lords Inn — probably a unique name. The sign is attractive, depicting Elizabethan nobles in fine costume. The building marks the common meeting point of estates belonging to Edgcumbe, Rashleigh, Carlyon and Treffry — all local landowners and hence the name. The church dedicated to St Blaize stands slightly above the Cornish Arms at the bottom of the same hill. St Blaize is not a Cornish saint's name, but in mediaeval times wool was as important as tin in this area, and he is the patron saint of woolcombers in the town that was once a port. Beside the Pack Horse Inn, a short distance away, a solid building standing four square to the road was the wool market. Now neither tin nor wool finds its way here, and by the traffic lights only the Shell House remains as an interesting reminder of St Blazey's great days as a port. Par is its replacement perhaps, the port reclaimed from the sea by Joseph Austen who became Joseph Treffry. His finest achievement was the massive viaduct across the Luxulyan Valley, unbelievably beautiful in bluebell time. A left-hand turn before the St Blazey level crossing, then first right leads to one of Cornwall's loveliest places, with numerous walks through

Charlestown Museum and Visitors' Centre
Near car park
History of shipwrecks and rescues.
Displays of material from wrecks.

Treffry Viaduct
Luxulyan Valley SX 056572
Built for mineral railway and
aqueduct (1839), spanning valley
100ft high.

Roche Rock
Rocky outcrop south-east of village
with ruins of St Michael's Chapel,
licensed 1409.

Mid-Cornwal Craft Centre
Biscovey A390
Fine collection of craft and painting
in skilfully converted school.

Wheal Martyn China Clay Museum
Carthew
Open-air museum based on restored
clay works dating from about 1880.

Water wheel at Wheal Martyn China Clay Museum

the woods. Even the viaduct does not detract from Luxulyan's beauty and standing proud still, though unused, this rail, road and water bridge seems almost part of the woodland scene.

The narrow lane winds to the village, up and up between stone-littered fields. Overlooking Tregarden quarry, source of its building stone, Luxulyan's church centres the handsome cottages, all prepared to endure.

Everywhere beyond are white 'mountains' and at Roche (pronounced as in 'poach') the scene is unparalleled. But in this village the Rock rises like a mute guardian.

Nearby is St Dennis, its church set within an Iron Age encampment. Near Carthew on the A391 only two miles from St Austell is Wheal Martyn Museum, a unique open-air museum based on a restored clay pit. Displays, artifacts, books, pottery and a slide programme add to the interest.

3 Around Truro

About 2,500 years ago the first inhabitants settled here on the ridge above the water. Celts then established themselves, but not till 1140 was there any building of importance. This was a Norman castle, but only its name remains, as Castle Hill, the site of the weekly cattle market.

The tin trade brought wealth to Truro, and it was one of the earliest stannary towns to hold a charter, granted by Edward I in 1307. King John built a Coinage Hall in 1200 but this was demolished in the early nineteenth century. The Black Death (1348) halved the population, causing such poverty that the government remitted all taxes. During the Civil War, Prince Charles and Royalist troops were quartered here, and for a while Truro was also the temporary home of the Royal Mint.

In the eighteenth century the town was as fashionable as Bath, and among the cultural activities were a Philharmonic Society, Library and Book Society. The first of these still gives about thirty concerts a year.

Many gracious buildings were erected. The Assembly Rooms by the Cathedral have a fine facade worthy of attention, as is Ralph Allen Daniell's Mansion House in Prince's Street. He was nephew to Ralph Allen of St Blazey, and wealthy enough to use Bath stone and have the oak specially carved by craftsmen from the French prisoner of war camp at Penryn. The date 1792 is engraved on the roof. Merchants like William Lemon built elegant houses on both sides of Lemon Street, named after him, and looking down on them is a monument to Richard Lander. He discovered the source of the Niger and in 1830 was the first holder of the Royal Geographical Society's Gold Medal.

The ordinary houses, too, are worth more than a passing glance. Look for strangely-shaped roofs, old porticos, decorated facades, narrow, pointed windows and emotive names like Tanyard Court, Tippett's Backlet, Pydar Street and Coombes Lane — recalling the great days of Truro's wool trade. St Nicholas Street may not seem unusual, but here the merchants' houses and warehouses were cheek by jowl with the Guildhall of St Nicholas, probably extending across Boscawen Street down to Lemon Quay itself. The present car park is where ships berthed, while waiting for their cargoes. Today at the quay, across the A39, pleasure boats berth in the summer and run weekday boat trips down the Fal.

Most Cornish towns have narrow passages between houses. These are 'opes' — pronounced 'ops'. Truro is no exception and Squeezeguts Alley is perhaps the smallest and most awkward; Cathedral Lane, unexpectedly, is another.

The Prince of Wales laid the foundation stone of the cathedral on 20 May 1880. It was the first to be built in England since St Paul's. Truro, however, had become a city in 1877 when Bishop Benson was enthroned in St Mary's Parish Church, which was later demolished, except for the south aisle, which was incorporated into the new building. The three spired towers are interesting in their dedications. The central one (Victoria) was given in 1901 as a memorial for the Queen's life, and nine years later another local benefactor gave the two western towers — Edward and Alexandra. Altogether an unusual building, its Gothic style gives the city a continental look.

Truro is small compared with other cities, but it needs time to explore it fully. The Pannier Market is an exciting place — the cheese stall being exceptionally good — and adjoining shops have their own specialities. Pottle's provides good food, while in New Bridge Street the Bear Essential is more than a restaurant with a catchy name. It is a link with the days when the

Bear Inn was probably a centre for bear-baiting during the seventeenth and eighteenth centuries.

There is much to see in the Royal Institution of Cornwall which is both an art gallery and a museum. On display is a variety of material connected with life in the county since earliest times, the mining section being unusually fine. During the summer season there is generally an exhibition of special interest.

Nearby in Chapel Hill there is the Truro and Old Kiln Museum, the oldest pottery in Cornwall. It is open all the year from Monday to Saturday and visitors are welcome to watch craftsmen

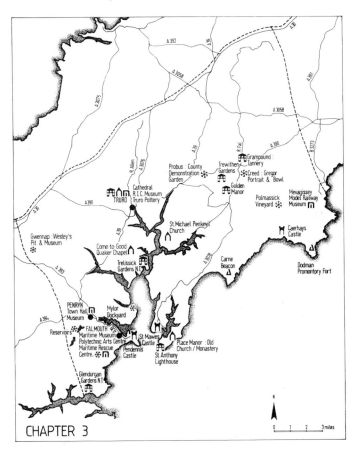

CHAPTER 3

Waterwheel at Wheal Martyn
China Clay Museum

China clay waste, St Austell

Wheel Inn, Tresillian

opposite its handsome clock tower are
The Manor and Cornwall's only bark
tannery. Here visitors are welcomed —
but only by appointment — this is the
place which provided skin for the hull
and sails of Tim Severin's curragh *St
Brendan*. This weathered a force eight
gale and crossed the Atlantic safely in
1976 — a feat which proved the theory
of the author-historian captain who
believed that St Brendan made the same
crossing in an identical craft a thousand
years before Columbus.

The second turning on the right up the
hill out of Grampound winds narrowly
to St Ewe, beautiful and almost unspoilt.
The church enclosed by trees, and the
old stocks in front of it, are both
interesting. The lane leads down to
Polmassick; after crossing the bridge, a
few yards past the chapel is another of
Cornwall's unexpected delights — a

vineyard where English wines are
available. There are walks round the
vineyard and the nearby farm.

Through Kestle one comes to
Mevagissey, one of the county's oldest
fishing ports. Its narrow streets and
quaint shops, up the hills or by the
quays, make it a captivating place.
Watch the gulls and the fishing boats, or
go fishing. If it rains, there is always the
Model Railway to enjoy. There is
pleasure here for the whole family. The
road south to Porthmellon hugs the cliff
before dipping down to the cove famous
for Percy Mitchell — the self-taught
boat designer, who started his shipyard
in 1924 and constructed everything from
a seven-foot dinghy to vessels of over
thirty tons. An artist in wood, he built
the *Windstar* for Sir Philip Hunloke,
Sailing Master to the Queen's father, as
well as various boats for the Admiralty.

Take care along the narrow winding road — summer traffic can be dangerous.

The coastal path to Gorran Haven passes Chapel Point — another spot associated with Tristan; he was imprisoned in the chapel, but leapt from a window to the safety of a rocky ledge — so the story goes. Walkers can enjoy fine views here. Gorran Haven itself is unexpectedly small but opens out into a wide bay.

Dodman Point, now a National Trust property, has a circular walk, starting and ending at the Penare car park. At the extreme point is a huge granite cross, erected in 1896 as a mark for seamen by the Vicar of Caerhays. After dedicating the cross, he kept a night's vigil beneath it, praying for the souls of shipwrecked mariners.

Hemmick Beach has no car park — only a narrow lane beside the water. It is quiet here and there is more than one stretch of sand. The lanes leading to it are dangerous, and care is essential to reach Porthluney Cove. There is a large car park and looking down over the beach is John Nash's Gothic building — Caerhays Castle. A fairytale place, it is

---

Places of Interest in the Veryan Area

County Demonstration Garden
Probus
Sectional gardens may be inspected, and there is an adviser on duty each Thursday afternoon.

Grampound Tannery
Cornwall's only bark tannery.
Visitors should telephone St Austell 882413, before visiting.

Polmassick Vineyard
St Ewe
A thriving vineyard, planted on the slopes of the Luney valley. Wines and vines for sale.

Model Railway and Museum
Mevagissey
In this fishing port an unusual attraction offering a miniature world of nearly fifty trains. Collection of model locomotives and rolling stock.

Dodman Point
Given to National Trust in 1919; a well-preserved Iron Age fort with baulk, ditch and rampart, crosses the neck of the headland. Granite cross erected as mark for seamen.

Caerhays Castle
A picturesque mansion built by John Nash for J.B. Trevanion (1808). Fine displays of shrubs in early spring. Gardens open twice in the year.

Creed Church
1m Grampound
Rebuilt in 1734 and retaining some of its wagon roof. Portrait of William Gregor and photograph of a titanium bowl near organ.

Golden Manor (SW 920469)
On private farm land is one of Cornwall's finest mediaeval barns. Can be seen without trespassing.

Trewithen Gardens
Probus
Privately owned, twenty acres, and internationally famous for rare shrubs.
Open on summer afternoons. Shrubs on sale.

Carne Barrow SW 913386
Cornwall's largest tumulus, thought to be the burial mound of King Geraint.

scorned by some, but loved by all when the rhododendrons are in bloom.

The Grampound road, after climbing past Caerhays church and Tubb's Mill, turns right along more narrow winding lanes to Creed. William Gregor was born not far from here in 1761. During his incumbency of the parish, he discovered titanium in black sand sent to him from Manaccan. It has been called manaccanite and gregorite, but is now universally accepted as titanium. In this secluded church there is a photograph of a titanium bowl and also a portrait of William Gregor.

From the Tregony road out of Creed the right-hand turn goes over the Fal to Golden Mill and Manor. Although this is a privately-owned farm, it is possible to drive as far as the main building without trespassing. The great barn on the left still has the fine windows and sturdy walls of a mediaeval hall. In 1577 Francis Tregian and his family lived here and offered shelter to Cuthbert Mayne (canonised in 1974). As they were known recusants, their property was searched, Mayne was discovered and executed, and Francis Tregian was condemned to a long period of imprisonment. Somehow he survived, went to Spain and died there in 1608. There are elegant memorials in Probus church to the Tregians and the Wolvedons (Golden is the Cornish mutation of this name).

A different kind of country house is nearby on the A390 at Trewithen. It was the seventeenth century home of the Hawkins family, but is now an internationally famous garden covering twenty acres.

The Roseland Peninsula includes the west side of Veryan Bay and Gerrans Bay, involving a long but very lovely drive. Take the A3078 where it turns off the A39 between Tresillian and Probus. It crosses the Tregony bridge where the left turn leads up to the now quiet village with its wide central street. This was once a bustling port and had a castle, a mediaeval market and a thriving wool factory. Even when the river silted up and trade declined, it was still a society meeting place. In the late nineteenth century, the learned Powder Book Club held meetings there for the improvement of local ladies, but no such excitements now remain. Little is left of former glories except the fourteenth-century church of St Cuby, with its slate tower and the handsome seventeenth-century clock tower which was rebuilt in 1895. The village now is a place of the past.

From Tregony high-banked, narrow lanes lead to Portholland, a harbour of two coves, east and west. There is a fine cliff path to Portloe but motorists lose the view temporarily as the road takes the inland route to this tiny port, more used to horse and pony transport than motorised traffic. Parking halfway down the steep hill to the beach avoids unpleasant turns, but visitors to the comfortable seventeenth-century Lugger Inn will find a park beside it. This village loses the sun very quickly, lying in the shadow of Jacka and Manare Points, but it is a good place in the sunshine. Some land here is owned by the National Trust as well as a considerable area along the cliff to Nare Head, one of the walks being round the point from Caragloose to Camels Cove. At Kiberick Cove there is a small car park and a footpath to the secluded beach. Another walk from the same parking place is down the valley to Paradoe Cove beyond the Nare, returning via that fine headland — one of the least known in Cornwall.

Veryan is well-known but still relatively unspoilt. The reasons for its fame are the unique round houses at each end of the village. Some say that a local vicar built them to keep the devil out, and away from his daughters. Whatever the reason, the white, thatched cottages have a charm all of their own. An interesting art gallery at the north end is worth visiting. Inside the church, with its unusual dedication to St Symphorian, lies Admiral Kempe, notable for sailing round the world with Cook and scaling Quebec Heights with General Wolfe. After passing Crugillick Manor on the way to the A3078, there is a walk or drive down the lovely wooded valley to Pendower Beach, another National Trust property. A disused lime-kiln is an interesting feature of this pleasant place. The great tumulus (Cornwall's largest) at nearby Carne Beacon is said to be the burial mound of King Geraint, who built Dingerin Castle where the Gerrans road leaves the A3078. It is believed that his tribesmen rowed his body, in a golden boat with silver oars, across the bay, to be burned and buried at Carne.

The church, art gallery and Cherry Tree Restaurant at Gerrans village offer different, but equally good, attractions for visitors. From here is a walk of about four miles along the coastpath to St Anthony Head, the eastern arm of Falmouth harbour. This superb route offers unsurpassed panoramic views on every side, until reaching Zone Point and the lighthouse. The headland has been fortified since Napoleonic days, was under military occupation during World War II, and then bought by the National Trust in 1959.

There is a splendid and easy coastal walk round the point to Place. Behind the Manor Hotel is the church of St Anthony, wrapped in legend. Tradition says that this was once a Celtic monastery whose history is written between the two rows of dog teeth on the south door. A rough translation of it is

that Christ visited this peninsula when his uncle, Joseph of Arimathea, came to trade for tin. When they were off St Anthony Head, a storm blew up and they sheltered in the little bay below Place Manor. While making the ship seaworthy again, they camped here, leaving a shrine behind them. Some years afterwards a church was built on the site. Apart from the legend, here is quiet beauty; the hotel is open from mid-May to September.

A delightful walk from Bohortha Farm to picturesque Froe overlooks Percuil and at the head of Froe inlet the water almost makes this headland an island. The journey back to Truro along the A3078 and A39 is about twenty miles, but the views of the Carrick Roads for most of the way make the mileage worthwhile.

The last exploration of the Roseland peninsula is shorter, and could last either an afternoon or a day. In early July, a signpost at Tresillian Bridge invites fruitlovers to pick strawberries at Fentongollan Farm, a pleasant task in good weather, as the farm is set high over woodlands and rolling fields. Follow the road to St Michael Penkevil — a handful of cottages round the church with the great gates of Tregothnan proclaiming it as private property. On certain days in early summer, Lord and Lady Falmouth open their gardens for charity. Visitors will enjoy the magnificent shrubs and see some of the mansion's 365 windows.

In 1319 the church was an important archpresbytery, (a college with four chaplains). An interesting feature is the second altar, on the upper floor of the tower, in accordance with an old tradition in churches dedicated to St Michael. Leaving the churchtown, take the first lane on the right through beautiful Lamorran woods, which lead

View from St Anthony headland

to Ruan Lanihorne. This is a haven for birdwatchers, and there is also a four-mile walk beside the river, where ships once sailed to Tregony.

There are walks to Philleigh where Glebe Country House (an elegant slate-hung Queen Anne mansion) offers tea — home-produced food, and scones hot from the oven with an abundance of cream, rarely found in Cornwall.

Resist the temptation to drive straight to King Harry Ferry — leave that until later — but watch the last times of sailing! Go on to St Just-in-Roseland where the church, in its creekside setting of tropical trees, is possibly unrivalled for beauty of position. At the water's edge of St Just Pool are workshops where items such as ships' figureheads or specialised work for the QEII have been produced.

The A3078 eventually reaches St Mawes Castle and drops down into the village to follow the harbour round for the return journey. This sheltered place is a yachting paradise, particularly for the wealthy. St Mawes Castle, cared for by the Department of the Environment, is a round tower, built by Henry VIII, and probably enlarged by his son Edward in 1550. (Its name is believed to have come from the hermit, St Mawes, St Mauditus or St Mause, who effected cures with the water from a holy well.) It is small but interesting, with ample parking. The grounds are pleasant — an ideal place to picnic and watch the various activities on the Carrick Roads.

On the way back to King Harry Ferry, make a detour to Turnaware Point. Here, in late summer, Cornwall's best blackberries grow abundantly. Its historical interest is that it was one of the places in Cornwall from which American troops sailed for Dunkirk in 1944.

Nearby, at the water's edge, Tolverne's thatched Smuggler's Cottage is interesting. Contraband was delivered here in the past, and there was still a ferry to Tregothnan Deer Park at the end of the nineteenth century; it was another point of departure for World War II troop carriers. Ruined Tolverne Chapel was built by Henry VI, who also established the ferry to Trelissick, which is still in use. Tales of Henry VIII riding with Ann Boleyn across this reach of the Fal on their honeymoon may be romantic, but they are not true.

The latest craft, launched in 1974, glides smoothly across the Fal to another delightful National Trust property. It is lovely at all seasons and the superb views include vistas of the estuary and Falmouth harbour. The Trust has made a four-mile nature trail round the grounds. The gardens are open to the public from April to October.

The thatched Punch Bowl and Ladle Inn at Penelewey dates from the eleventh century and is probably the only one with such a name. Cowlands Creek and Coombe are worth a detour to enjoy the birds, the creekside walks and the famous Kea plums.

The lane joins the A39 Falmouth to Truro road at Calenick, once the site of Cornwall's chief smelting house. All that remains of it is the handsome clock tower on the slatehung Bridge House.

The great men of Truro made fortunes in tin during the eighteenth and nineteenth centuries, but it had been 'streamed' in the surrounding districts long before Truro became an important trading centre; so it is interesting to look at those old mining areas. The Truro to

---

Places of Interest on the St Mawes Peninsula

St Michael Penkevil Church
Restored 1863-5, a handsome building. Altar inside the tower's upper floor.

St Mawes Castle
Described as Henry VIII's most decorative fort. Colourful gardens and lawns to the sea.

Trelissick (National Trust)
Only gardens open, with fine shrubs and nature trails.

St Anthony Lighthouse
Built 1835, open to visitors. Headland has been fortified since Napoleonic times.

Place Church
St Anthony-in-Roseland
Behind the Manor Hotel lies a church built on the site of an early Celtic monastery — the Priory and Convent of St Mary-de-Valle.

Falmouth A39 road down Arch Hill goes under the track of a mineral railway before climbing the hill to Playing Place — once the site of a theatre in the round. Carnon Downs looks like a bungalow suburb, but hides much mining history. By the village shop, a road turns left for Come-to-Good, a misleading name which has quite a different meaning. The thatched Quaker Meeting House of 1710 is called after its location *Cwm-ty-quite* — Cornish for 'the House of the Coombe in the Woods', appropriate for this attractive building still in use.

Feock church has an interesting lychgate with a slate-hung upper storey, and expensive properties beyond the village straggle down to Restronguet Point beside the Carrick Roads. Before Tudor times a passenger ferry, which functioned at the turn of this century, took travellers from Truro through Mylor to Penryn and Falmouth. Across the narrow water is the thatched Pandora Inn, which was originally called The Ship. It was bought by a captain whose ship had formed part of Captain Bligh's expedition to capture the *Bounty* mutineers. On the return voyage, the captain's ship foundered, and though he returned with some prisoners, he was dismissed from the service. He renamed the inn Pandora after his lost ship.

At Point, Restronguet Creek is joined by the Carnon River, a bird sanctuary and a place of beauty. Once it was a prosperous mining port with a reputation for smuggling as well. Tin has been streamed in the Carnon River since the days of pre-history, and in the Middle Ages ore from inland mines was brought here for export on mules and horses. In 1826 the Redruth and Chacewater Railway opened, the stretch from Devoran to Point still retaining horse-drawn wagons: and part of this track can still be seen. Great Scandinavian schooners anchored there, unloading timber which was taken upstream on barges to Perran Wharf for distribution to the mines. The name of the Norway Inn is a reminder of those. There are remains of these industrial buildings at Devoran, for all the stone bollards and wooden wharves have not yet disappeared. The old weighbridge gate still exists beside the cottage at the junction where the Bissoe road leaves the A39.

Beyond the Norway, a road winds away to Perranwell — here the name PERRAN FOUNDRY (1799) is clearly visible on the front of Bibby's Store and recalls the days when the Fox family established their foundry. The machinery was of high quality and was

---

Places of Interest in the Mining Area near Truro

Quaker Chapel
Come-to-Good
Friends' Meeting House, attractively thatched — still in use.

Wesley's Pit and Museum
Busveal, Redruth
Each Whit Monday Methodists gather here for a celebratory service. (Information obtainable from Mr Tom Shaw — Redruth 212104.)

---

used throughout the world: they supplied the world's largest steam engine to drain the Haarlem Meer in the Netherlands.

Beyond Perranwell and Frogpool, Gwennap village lies in peaceful beech woods, deceptively quiet now, yet once the heart of a region which yielded more copper and tin than any other place in the Old World. Gwennap Pit is not in the village, but is near Busveal, reached by turning off the A393 Falmouth to Redruth road at the Fox and Hounds — one of the many inns where a service is held and produce auctioned for charity at harvest time.

The road twists and climbs above the derelict expanse of the now silent mines: Crofthandy, Goon Gumpus, Creegbrawse, Tolgullow and others with Celtic names. The men who worked there often died young and left young widows with families. Others fell ill and were unable to work. Wesley's message from the Pit and elsewhere brought hope to these people; as he wrote 'The more I converse with the believers in Cornwall, the more I am convinced that they have sustained great loss for want of hearing the doctrine of Christian Perfection clearly and strongly enforced.' Gwennap Pit was probably formed by the collapse

of underground mining excavations. In 1806 circular terraces were cut for seating, and since 1807 an annual service has been held there on Whit Monday. Wesley writes of preaching in a hollow capable of containing many thousand people. Gwennap Pit is certainly large; it was central and ideal for his purpose whether it held hundreds or thousands. A Museum of Cornish Methodism was opened here in 1982.

Carharrack is a village of sad mining memories, but St Day has a different story to tell. Prosperous mine owners and captains lived there and perhaps its real place in Cornwall's history is its role as one of the rests for pilgrims en route to St Michael's Mount. Today, living precariously over a honeycomb of mines, in August it welcomes modern pilgrims to the St Day Walsingham Festival, which is held for those unable to travel to the Norfolk shrine.

Killifreth engine house is undoubtedly one of the most impressive industrial buildings remaining. It is near Scorrier, where John Williams, the mining entrepreneur built his fine mansion. Not quite two miles north-east along the A30 is Blackwater, birthplace of John Passmore Edwards, who built reading rooms and institutes for all workers — especially miners. His Reading Room there stands beside the main road; almost every town in Cornwall owes its library to him. Altogether he was responsible for fifty-three benefactions, from Newlyn to Dundee.

This section of the A30 has three important tumuli beside it, Two Burrows, Three Burrows and Four Burrows; and one of the Midsummer Eve Bonfire ceremonies by members of the Old Cornwall Society usually takes place at the last of these. From the A390 at Chacewater, minor roads lead to Baldhu (Black Mine) and Wheal Jane Mine, re-opened in 1970 as a modern mining complex. The surrounding area is one where mineral enthusiasts can explore ochre pits, arsenic works and similar remains. From here to Truro by way of the winding lanes of Penweathers there are walks and picnic places, but few people.

Before reaching Penryn and Falmouth, turn left from the A39 immediately after the Norway Inn. This leads to Mylor, much sought after by yachtsmen. The steep lane which winds away from the traffic is known locally as 'Craft and Danger' — an interesting corruption of *croft an D'Angers* (D'Angers' fields). This must have described it in 1154, when the uncultivated hillside belonged to the Norman from Angers who owned the barton of Crueglew (the enclosed land by the prehistoric barrow). The wealthy mining engineer William Lemon of Breage bought the estate in 1749; its name was then Carclew. The house became one of the cultural centres of Cornwall. The Lemons were great benefactors to the people of Mylor: Sir Charles bought the workhouse, converted it into a school and maintained it for years. Fire unfortunately destroyed the manor house, but Carclew Gardens are occasionally open to the public. The Lemon name died out and became Tremayne, but is perpetuated in the village in the Lemon Arms and Lemon Hill.

Mylor Bridge is at the head of the creek, but the original settlement was the churchtown at its mouth a mile away. In the mid-nineteenth century the buildings by the pier were known as HMS *Ganges*, at that time the Royal Navy's only shore-based training centre and hospital. The ship, however, was anchored at St Just Pool across the Carrick Roads. Today it is a yachting centre, but the restaurant there still bears the old name.

Almost hidden in trees, beside the water stands St Mylor Church, a picturesque building with a separate bell tower and Cornwall's tallest cross embedded in the ground at the south door. One of the churchyard epitaphs is unusual and visitors are told to read about 'Joseph Crapp, a shipwright who died ye 26th of November 1770, aged 43 years'. His death is graphically described:

Alas friend Joseph
His end was almost sudden
As though a mandate came
Express from Heaven
His foot, it slip and he did fall
Help, help he cries, and that was all.

Inside, the carved wood of the pulpit is believed to have come from Armada wrecks, but the choir screen recalls more recent events. It was given in memory of those drowned in 1966 when an overloaded local pleasure boat capsized.

The writer Howard Spring found this creek so enchanting that he moved here in 1939 and used it as the background for his bestselling novel *All The Day Long*. The walk round Trefusis Point has views of Falmouth Bay — perhaps the finest natural harbour in the world.

The walk ends at Flushing, meeting the road from Mylor. Its Celtic name was Nankersey, but when Dutch engineers arrived to build Falmouth's quays, they settled here and changed the name to remind them of their homeland. The cottages cling to the waterside, and the village is reputed to have the mildest climate in the country. Flowers bloom here all the year round as if endorsing that claim. In the nineteenth century, the great days of Packet ships, it was a fashionable place to live. Lord Exmouth was born here, and Lord Buckingham dined and wined with other society notables. Today sailors are there for pleasure, not national business, as were the men of former days.

There is no bus from here, and the ferry across to Falmouth is the quickest way out of the village. At the head of the river is Penryn, reached either by a waterside path or inland road. These ways meet at the bottom of the steep hill beside St Gluvias, the parish church of Penryn. The town, in fact, grew from a settlement on the hill across the river. It has an interesting history, part splendid, part sad, but cherishes hopes for the future. Founded as a borough in 1216, it was granted a charter in 1236 and saw the rise and fall of Glasney Collegiate Church from 1265 to 1549. This establishment was a centre for religious instruction, growing in importance as Penryn's trade increased.

The closure of Glasney at the Dissolution, however, followed by the unexpected rise of Falmouth at the mouth of the river, led to a decline from which Penryn has never really recovered. But in 1977 its unique mediaeval character was recognised as rare, and Government grants were given to save old buildings, initiating a programme of conservation. As a result, the town whose granite is to be seen in buildings as different as London's Thames Embankment, the harbour of Singapore and Fastnet lighthouse, is fast becoming a tourist attraction. A place to visit is the Town Hall Museum; once the gaol, it now houses a variety of interesting items connected with Penryn's history.

In Tudor times, the Fal River saw more shipping than any other port in the kingdom, and Henry VIII, concerned about possible Spanish attacks, built Pendennis Castle (now in the care of the Department of the Environment). It commands Falmouth's best views: on one side, the holiday beaches, on the other, the docks and the town. This point is ideal for a coastguard station and one of the most modern, the Maritime Rescue Co-ordination Centre, was opened in 1981 by Prince Charles. Visitors are told about the service that operates across the Atlantic and to the Spanish border.

In the coaching days, the Green Bank Hotel was important. In the early years of this century, Kenneth Grahame began his *Wind in the Willows* here — proof of this is framed in the lobby. Down High Street — much changed since a disastrous fire in the last century — and to the left, is the Prince of Wales Pier where the Flushing ferry disembarks its passengers. It is also the berth for numerous pleasure boats. The Moor lies above Market Strand and deceives most people with its name. From the bottom of Jacob's Ladder, (111 steps) boatmen used to ferry people over, and moor outside the Seven Stars. This small building (dated 1610) is where generations of innkeepers have drawn beer from the wood — a tradition continued today. The granite obelisk in the centre of the Moor is a memorial to men of the Packet Service when 'Falmouth for Orders' was the command obeyed by all captains of these ships. For over two and a half centuries, the Packets carried mail, cargoes and passengers to many parts of the world.

Walking through the town is a casual affair, traffic usually giving way to pedestrians. In Church Street is the Falmouth Arts Centre, where, in the early nineteenth century, the Fox family of Quakers established the Polytechnic Society and reading rooms, setting a trend later followed throughout the country. At the far end of the town is the Georgian Custom House, handsome with its Greek Doric columns and fine facade. Beside and below, the King's

Places of Interest around Penryn and Falmouth

Mylor Dockyard
Now Yacht Club and sailing centre, in 1866 it was HMS *Ganges,* naval training dockyard.

Penryn Town Hall and Museum
Standing centrally on Penryn's spine road, it houses offices and museum of local history.

Falmouth Polytechnic Arts Centre
Church Street
Formed in 1833 at suggestion of the Quaker Anna Maria Fox 'to promote useful arts'. Later copied all over Britain.

Falmouth Maritime Museum
Custom House Quay
Appropriately in the tug *St Denys;* unusual maritime exhibits. It has a unique engine.

Argal and College Reservoirs
B3291 Penryn-Constantine road
Pleasant recreational areas, ideal for walking.

Pendennis Castle
Falmouth
A well preserved castle built by Henry VIII in 1539-43 shortly after Little Dennis blockhouse below. Enlarged by Elizabeth I, and besieged successfully by Fairfax during the Civil War.

The Maritime Rescue Co-ordination Centre
Pendennis Point
This purpose-built coastguard station was opened by Prince Charles in December 1981. Officials co-ordinate search and rescue round coastline of Great Britain and (Northern) Ireland. In 1982 Falmouth was first Centre in eastern Atlantic to answer calls in the MARISAT satellite system. Visitors are welcome — Telephone Falmouth 314269 (District Controller) first.

Glendurgan Gardens (National Trust)
Valley gardens of great beauty, best seen in spring — flowering shrubs. Runs to Durgan village on Helford River. A maze and pool are attractive.

Custom House Quay, Falmouth

Pipe is an interesting reminder of the manner in which contraband tobacco used to be destroyed. Appropriately moored at this conservation area of Custom House Quay, and now housing Falmouth's Maritime Museum, is the steam tug St Denys. It is a small vessel but gives visitors a true naval atmosphere, reflecting the history of the town. Opposite Arwenack House is the waterside granite obelisk erected in 1738 by Martin Lister Killigrew as a memorial to his wife's family. They had lived at Arwenack and founded Falmouth, which evolved from Sir Walter Raleigh's plan to develop the harbour. He had stayed at Arwenack with the Killigrews and urged them to press forward with the project. By 1613, in spite of objections from Penryn, the town's identity had been formulated, and Falmouth was born.

The view over the docks from Castle Drive is one no visitor should miss. With the background of Trefusis Point and the Roseland Peninsula this busy area is probably unique, and there are hopes for a prosperous future as a result of oil explorations in the Celtic Sea.

Round the headland the road leads to Castle Beach, Gyllyngvase and, beyond, to Swanpool and Maenporth. These are beautiful beaches with sands and rock pools to keep children happy for the whole holiday. Swanpool — as its name implies — is something else as well;

rowing boats and canoes often share the waters with a variety of birds.

Nearby are Penjerrick Gardens, a Fox property now opened to the public. Spring time is the best for a visit here — when the flowering shrubs are a mass of colour. From the beaches the coast path goes to Rosemullion Head, but motorists are restricted to the road which ends at Mawnan church. It was built on an Iron Age site, its tower warning seamen that they were near the dreaded Manacle Rocks. Over the lych gate an inscription in Cornish reads: *Da thym ythyn nesse the Thu* — which means 'It is good for me to draw nigh unto the Lord'. Inside is a wide variety of colourful tapestry kneelers — the choir's are patterned with mediaeval tunes.

Round the headland lies Durgan, a tiny village reached by cliff path or road via Mawnan Smith. Here are only a handful of cottages beside a small beach (partly owned by the National Trust) with safe bathing. Glendurgan Gardens above are also owned by the Trust and open, but not the house, which is occupied by the Fox family.

Beside the B3291 Penryn road is the Military Vehicle Museum at Lamanva.

Under all-weather cover, its exhibits include British and American fighting vehicles, badges, medals and equipment. Argal and Penryn College reservoirs nearby have much to offer.

On the right of the lanes to Stithians is the Rosemanowes Quarry. Here successful dry, hot, rock experiments have been carried out by the Camborne School of Mines. The church is screened by trees, but not the hotel, which offers excellent carvery meals.

St Stythians Feast and the Agricultural Show are held in the second week in July. Second only to the Royal Cornwall Show, farmers come 'home' from all over the world for this event. It was first held in 1834 to stimulate competition between farmers when agriculture was at a low ebb. It is still a very local show.

From here a secondary road climbs to overlook Kennal Vale and Ponsanooth. The sign 'Kennal Mills' is a reminder of the former prosperity from gunpowder and from the woollen mills when they were in full production. Below the viaduct are the Halancoose Nurseries. To the right lies Falmouth, to the left Carnon Downs and Truro.

4 Helston and The Lizard

About halfway between Truro and Penzance is Helston, an historic town apparently oblivious of the A394 traffic which divides it. But on 8 May each year the past takes over, as old houses and twisting streets echo with Flora Day celebrations — once a pagan welcome to spring. Legend links the occasion with St Michael and the devil, who tore the lid off hell in a final effort to defeat his enemy. An inaccurate aim sent the stone elsewhere and till 1783 it was to be seen embedded in the courtyard of The Angel Hotel. Great celebrations followed and the townsfolk adopted the saint as their patron. Whatever the truth, this annual event is worth seeing, particularly the noon dance when couples in morning dress pick up the words of the song played by a local band and dance literally 'in and out of the houses'.

Helston's 1305 Charter ruled that tinners should bring their mineral here for coinage or testing. Below the old Grammar School, where Charles Kingsley was educated, Coinagehall Street is an echo of mediaeval days. The church at the back of the town is behind the Guildhall and the Buttermarket Museum. Neither of these should be missed, particularly the latter, which has a good display of folk history that includes Henry Trengrouse's life-saving rocket — invented after the *Anson* shipwreck on Loe Bar. Fresh fish and craft shops in Meneage Street are of above average quality, as is Monday's cattle market at the lower end of the town.

The B3304 passes the boating pool on the Porthleven Road but walkers and

---

Places of Interest in Helston

Angel Hotel
Partly sixteenth century, at the end of the seventeenth it became the town house of Sidney Godolphin.

Guildhall
In 1576 a market house was built here and incorporated the Town Hall. Later a Corn Market was held here.

Butter Market Museum
This is housed in the former Market House in Church Street. It was built in 1837-8 in two parts — one for butter and eggs, the other for meat.

Loe Pool (National Trust)
This freshwater lake is an unusual example of the 'drowned valleys' occurring in Devon and Cornwall. The Loe Bar formed by accumulated shingle from the Atlantic has dammed the former estuary which made the port of Helston. A five mile footpath runs round it and has small car parks at various points; excellent for birdwatching.

---

ornithologists will want to explore the grounds of Penrose beside Loe Pool, Cornwall's largest lake. There is easy parking at the two entrances and the six-mile walk taking in Loe Bar Sands will probably mean a rambling day and a picnic. Porthleven is a good place for tea, after wandering through its narrow streets and visiting Breageside. There is now an intriguing craft centre here, housed in a store originally built to hold

7,000 tons of china clay.

Off the A394 to Penzance, running almost parallel with the coast, several lanes lead to headlands and byways. Trewavas (Joseph Trewavas received Cornwall's first VC in 1856) and nearby Rinsey Head are ideal for picnics. Part of the area and the car park belong to the National Trust. Praa (Pray) Sands, a caravanners' haven, has a silver mile of dunes and safe beaches. Motorists can drive on to Acton Castle where Sandor Vegh held his Masterclasses, but there are only footpaths to Cudden Point with its unusual view of St Michael's Mount. Walkers will enjoy Prussia and Betsy's Cove, both haunts of John Carter, an

eighteenth-century smuggler and self-styled 'King of Prussia'.

The great inland mining area is reached via Goldsithney, once a busy place in coaching days, but now a quiet village. St Hilary Church — easy to see but hard to locate — is on an ancient Celtic site. It was sadly despoiled in 1932, but it remains open for those who want to see its present treasures.

Off the B3280 a turn to Godolphin Cross comes after the hamlets of Relubbus and Bosence, both busy, lively places in Roman times. Relubbus had the tide at its feet and Roman remains at Bosence prove its trading capabilities. Deep in woodland lies Godolphin, a

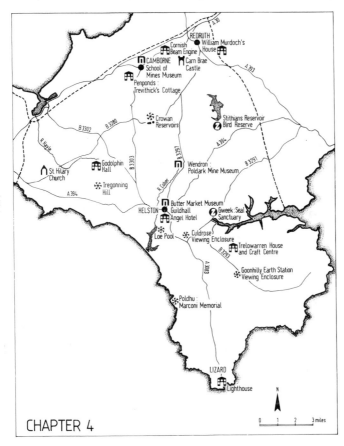

CHAPTER 4

Porthleven

house which deserves a book to itself. This fifteenth-century mansion, built with wealth from nearby mines, was used in the *Poldark* television series. Sir Sidney Godolphin, Elizabeth I's great High Treasurer, and the famed Godolphin Arab stallion are only part of the history associated with this property.

The whole area of Godolphin and Tregonning is ideal for walks and picnics, made more pleasant by easy roadside parking. Chief Conin's dwelling, Tregonning, is a hill of ancient settlements and of more recent interest for William Cookworthy's discovery of china clay there in 1746. His subsequent findings at Carloggas near St Austell eventually led to the formation of Cornwall's most modern industry.

Before returning to Helston, stop at Breage (pronounced as in 'vague') church. It contains Margaret Godolphin's coffin plate, a Roman milestone and some fine murals.

Three miles north of Helston along the B3297 is Wendron and the Poldark Mine. Here you can go safely underground, and experience for

yourself something of the past. Tin lodes, working machinery, and even dripping water help to recreate the mining age, with some of Richard Trevithick's instruments on display. Ample picnic space, inside and out, is available, and there are varied entertainments for the children. Allow plenty of time here.

North once more, the bleak Carnmenellis Moor emphasises the mining atmosphere and a short climb to Hangman's Barrow and the Nine Maidens stone circle adds still more. This, too, is a place of many walks. Nearby, Stithians Reservoir is a must for ornithologists, but, for access to the hide, they should first obtain permission from the Cornwall Bird Watching and Preservation Society.

Carnkie's disused engine houses have a melancholy beauty, best viewed first from the centre of the village and then, in panorama, from Carn Brea. Here is another place to visit whether you are artist, historian, birdlover or gourmet. Good coffee with home baking and full meals are served at the unique recently-

Trewavas Head

Places of Interest around Helston

St Hilary Church
Thirteenth-century tower, but the main building dates from 1854. Inscribed stone in churchyard probably sixth century. Unusual wall paintings inside.

Godolphin House
Breage
Fifteenth-century mansion three miles from Mounts Bay. Nearby Godolphin Hill mines provided source of family wealth.

Tregonning Hill
Ashton
Place of considerable pre-historic interest. William Cookworthy discovered the first china clay here in 1746. Ideal for picnics, with easy parking.

Poldark Mine
Wendron
A real mine to explore. Here is old machinery working. A museum also of mining exhibits, books and gifts.

Cornish Beam Engine (National Trust)
Pool
Working example of winding engine and pumping engine used at local copper and tin mines.

Camborne School of Mines Museum
Pool
On A3047 beyond the beam engine is the internationally famous School of Mines with a fine collection of minerals and rocks from Cornwall and many parts of the world.

Trelowarren House and Craft Centre
Mawgan-in-Meneage
Home of the Vyvyans since 1426. The Elizabethan style Stuart building has a Victorian interior — open during August. On the estate is a pottery and craft centre, and a caravan site.

Stithians Reservoir
Birdwatching, sailing, rowing, and other pursuits: permits needed, from the SWWA.

William Murdoch's House
Redruth
In Cross Street, Murdoch was the first to invent and use gas-lighting.

Richard Trevithick's Cottage
Lower Penponds (National Trust)
This interesting thatched cottage where the great engineer lived and worked for over thirty years. Not open to the public.

Crowan Reservoirs
Pleasant places beside the B3280 Redruth to Hayle road.

Cornish Seal Sanctuary
Gweek
First started in 1958 when Ken Jones cared for a day-old seal washed up at St Agnes. He now devotes his life to the welfare of these animals.

Royal Naval Air Station, Culdrose
A3083
One of Europe's largest stations, with machines always on standby. Public viewing enclosure near the car park.

Goonhilly Earth Station B3293
The huge dish scanners of the Post Office Earth Station can be seen from the pubic viewing enclosure.

Lizard Lighthouse
Built in 1751, altered in 1903. A squat building with white walls, cowls and foghorns.

Marconi Memorial
Poldhu
A small obelisk on the golf course near the hotel marks the place where the experiments of transatlantic radio transmissions were first successful.

restored castle. Come when gorse and heather are out, explore the top of the Brea, where you can sit and relax. There is a path to St Euny and Redruth Churchtown. Nearby Reswythen Bridge was made unstable in 1301 by the mining operations of Ralph Wenna and John de Treveyngy, and their goods were confiscated to pay for the damage. In Redruth, a good local history library is to be found just above Cross Street, where William Murdoch invented gas lighting in 1792.

Sir Richard Tangye (1833 - 1905) was born at Illogan and became a national benefactor and brilliant engineer. He instituted the Saturday half-holiday and built machinery that helped raise Cleopatra's Needle on the Embankment. His inspiration was Richard Trevithick (1771 -1833), the neglected genius who invented the first vehicle ever to travel literally 'under its own steam'. His statue outside Camborne Library faces the street where he first put his theories into practice.

Beside the main road at Pool is a Cornish 'whim' engine or steam winding engine, while just north of this is a huge Cornish beam engine. The whim raised copper ore from the East Pool Mine to the surface while the beam engine pumped water out of the workings. These two engines are now in the care of the National Trust.

Pool has a fine Leisure Centre — a good place to spend a day, enjoying sport or relaxing. The famous Camborne School of Mines is on the A30 and off the B3303 at Penponds is the cottage — now belonging to the National Trust — where Trevithick lived most of his life. Barriper (meaning Beau Repaire) road was once on the pilgrims' route to St Michael's Mount. A short detour to Gwinear enables one to visit the Miniature Railway there. On

returning via Leedstown, it is difficult to imagine that this was once a busy industrial region. Its un-Cornish name dates from 1740 when the youngest daughter of Sir Francis Godolphin married the Duke of Leeds. It is now quiet and Gwinear Downs are splendid for walks and picnics. A footpath runs close to the old mineral railway track which carried copper and tin ore to the port of Hayle.

William Oliver lived at Truthall, a finely preserved manor in Sithney parish. He later moved to Bath, and made famous the biscuits which still bear his portrait. The church has a fine collection of glass medallions believed to be from the thirteenth century.

From Helston the Lizard peninsula can be explored by turning off the A394 Falmouth road past Trewennack to Gweek. Pleasant high-hedged lanes lead to Boskenwyn Downs and open on to a straight road probably constructed by the Romans to take tin from Grambla to

Ken Jones at the Cornish Seal Sanctuary

St Keverne

narrower primrose-clad lane on the far side of the house offers rewards for brave motorists. It is narrow and steep, winding up past an ancient earthwork, dipping through beech and elm woods before crossing the B3293 to wander up and down into the valley of Mawgan-in-Meneage Church. The whole parish of Monks (Meneage or Menaig seems to come from Cornish Managh or Monk) is full of beauty and history — its church provides something of both. Look for the seventeenth-century sundial, a dog door and an unusual brass memorial to Hannibal Basset.

Keep to the Manaccan road through wooded lanes, until a signpost to Kestle is reached. This lane leads to the unbelievable haven of Frenchman's Creek, which Daphne du Maurier saw, loved and made famous in her book of the same name. It has rightly been described as a place of 'distinct, eerie charm', and access to it is close by the farm. Over thirty-five acres along the south bank are National Trust property; footpaths go to Tremayne Quay and Helford.

Motorists return to the Manaccan road for Helford to see the thatched beauty of that village, stop at the old Shipwrights' Arms and cross the river at Monks' Passage to the Ferryboat Inn. The road to Manaccan is a delight; so is the village, perched saucily on a hillside. Geologists will remember that William Gregor discovered titanium from here and all should note that ill luck befalls those who pick figs from the tree in the church wall. Few, however, may know that Bligh of the *Bounty* came here to survey for the Admiralty, was mistaken for a French spy, and promptly arrested. The centuries-old New Inn provides a wide variety of good food — beside a log fire.

St Anthony Church on the beach at

the port. Gweek's unusual name comes from the Latin *Vicus* — which confirms the Roman presence. Since very early times the valleys all round have been streamed for tin, and careful observers may still discover ancient tin moulds built into the quay walls. In 1201 Gweek was important enough to warrant a merchant guild as well as burgess privileges. The creek is now silted up and beside it is now a Seal Sanctuary; numerous birds enjoy the quiet, and donkeys graze happily in the adjoining meadows.

The B3293 to St Keverne runs between a thatched tollhouse and the water — a pretty road affording occasional glimpses of the creek and walks through the woods. But a

Mullion Cove

Gillan harbour is as beautiful as its surroundings. This was a busy port in mediaeval times, with ships sailing to Southampton loaded with fish, fish oil, hides, slate and tin. The remote village across the water is protected by a difficult access road; but walkers may follow the coastal path, as motorists have to turn inland again. The wild cliffs and fierce rocks explain the need for a coastguard and the lifeboat that was stationed here from 1869 - 1945, rescuing ships from the dreaded Manacles. Porthoustock (P'roustock) is a somewhat calmer place today, as local men find quarrying roadstone safer than fishing.

St Keverne church has reminders of shipwrecks and has rightly been called the church of heartbreak. A plaque on the churchyard wall is in memory of Michael Josef, whose fight against unjust taxes in 1497 led to his death at Tyburn; it is an undying memory in the hearts of all Cornishmen.

Before returning to Helston, stop at Trelowarren. This was the home of the Vyvyans for five hundred years, but is now used for conferences and retreats. It also has one of the most secluded caravan parks in the county, fine grounds to wander in, and an interesting craft shop which also sells good coffee.

Just outside Helston, off the main A3083 Lizard road is the Cornwall Aero Park where there is all-weather family entertainment, including many aspects of flying. A short way on, the Culdrose Royal Naval Air Station has a public viewing area.

The B3293 from here leads to Goonhilly Downs Earth Station, where dish-type aerials turn to the sky like creatures of science fiction. They were

Cadgwith

sited in this particular area because only a granite foundation is strong enough to bear the weight of these impressive structures.

From July to October these barren downs are brilliant with white-pink and deep lilac Cornish heather, rarely found elsewhere, part of the Lizard's unique flora. Adjoining the Station is a National Nature Reserve of 103 acres.

About four miles eastwards, the B3294 leads to Coverack, where there are cliff walks, a lifeboat station and a safe beach.

A fine coastal path leads from here to Kennack Sands, a good beach for swimming in calm weather. The motorist, however, must return to the B3293 and turn left at Traboe Cross, just before the Earth Station. Poltesco cove is reached by scrambling down beside a trout stream, but it is well worth the effort; look for Nature Trail signs. All

round is serpentine: great blocks were used for St Ruan's church tower and Grade church (found at the end of a cart track) has a two-storey serpentine and granite tower.

There are spectacular cliff walks from here to Cadgwith and Landewednack. Lizard light is Britain's most southerly beacon, and one of the world's most powerful. Lizard village is little more than a group of souvenir shops selling serpentine in varied forms.

Kynance Cove (National Trust, approached by a toll road) is a much-loved beauty spot, but access to it is steep. Mullion village church is fifteenth century, with excellent bench ends.

On the cliffs of Poldhu Cove is Guglielmo Marconi's memorial. From here in 1901 the first radio message crossed the Atlantic, and later the short-wave beam system was tested successfully.

5 Penzance and Land's End

Rail travellers have always thought of Penzance as the place of journey's end. It is certainly the rail terminus in the west but the locals say that it is in fact where Cornwall begins. Before exploring the area of West Penwith (*Penwyth* is the Cornish for extremity) to discover the truth of this statement, there is much to enjoy in the town of Penzance itself, for it is a place of surprises.

Beautiful still, with its high, stone-stepped pavement, is Market Jew Street, the main thoroughfare which greets pedestrians, motorists and rail travellers, who have left the station at the bottom of the hill. The long road leads to the handsome granite Town Hall before which stands the statue of Sir Humphry Davy. He was born in a house close by, where he began the experiments which

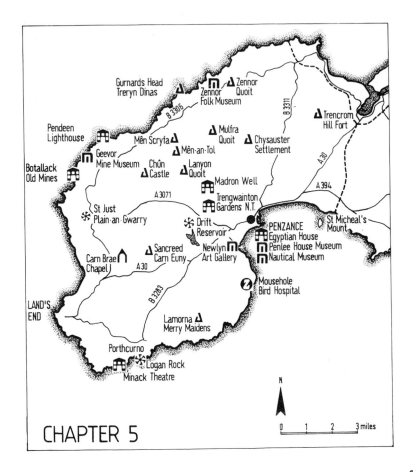

CHAPTER 5

eventually brought him fame. He was knighted in 1812 for his contributions to science, and later created baronet for his invention of the miner's safety lamp. It is perhaps not surprising that Davy, one of the foremost European chemists of the nineteenth century, was the one who realised and encouraged the talents of Michael Faraday. Davy's wide range of interests also touched on poetry as well as the natural sciences. President of the Royal Society at forty-one, founder of the Athenaeum Club and the London Zoo, this man of Penzance was worthy to be called a genius.

The road behind the Town Hall turns left towards the harbour and the Barbican Aquarium, down the quiet way that is Chapel Street. It is hard to realise that it once bustled with mule trains laden with their copper for ships' cargoes. Now it is a pleasant backwater of memories — many of them lingering in the Union Hotel, where the Battle of Trafalgar victory was first announced from the minstrels' gallery. Local fishermen had learnt it from the ship racing up channel to Falmouth with the news. Such was local pride in this 'first' that Penzance men made the Nelson banner (now in Madron Church) that has ever since been carried in procession on the Sunday nearest to Trafalgar Day. At the back of this historic building there is the shell of a Georgian theatre, opened in 1789.

The National Trust's Egyptian House in Chapel Street, with its flamboyant facade, is well worth seeing. Part of the ground floor is taken up by a National Trust shop. The Admiral Benbow Restaurant and Nautical Museum is at the sea end of this interesting street and is also worth a visit.

There are many side ways and shop-lined lanes to explore in this most western of Cornwall's towns. Each has

Places of Interest in Penzance

The Barbican
Harbour
A fine aquarium and craft workshops are among the attractions here. Fishing trips can be arranged.

The Egyptian House
Chapel Street
Worth seeing for the unusual facade. Built about 1830. Part let as holiday flats, but part National Trust shop.

Nautical Museum
Chapel Street
Varied, interesting, appropriate exhibits for this maritime place, with many items recovered, by diving, from historic wrecks.

Museum of the Royal Geological Society of Cornwall
Alverton Street
Exhibits include Cornish rocks, minerals and fossils mostly related to Cornwall's extractive industries.

Penlee Museum
Entirely local display reflecting the history and environment of Penzance.

something to offer, but beyond Market Jew Street the road leads on to Alverton, with the granite block of St John's, that houses the Royal Geological Museum and other items of interest.

Not far away is the Penlee House Museum and the Morrab Library — a place of many treasures standing in subtropical gardens where camellias bloom at Christmas above the long promenade stretching from Newlyn to the memorial at the end of Chapel Street.

From here the road follows the vast, magnificent sweep of Mount's Bay, past the heliport (for the Isles of Scilly) and Long Rock to Marazion, a place which has a fine view of the Mount, golden sands, safe bathing and marshes that attract birdwatchers.

Marazion was a thriving port as long ago as the Bronze Age; it was on one of the main overland routes for merchants taking Irish gold to Brittany. Legend tells that St Michael appeared to some hermits supposedly on a large rock which has ever since been known as St Michael's Chair. In fact it was Edward the Confessor who established a Benedictine Chapel here, and the monks' domestic buildings are now incorporated in the fourteenth-century castle on the rock summit. Even grey skies cannot dim the magical quality of the Mount, given by Lord St Levan to the National Trust in 1954. His son, the fourth Baron, now lives there. Visitors reach it by foot across a causeway, or by ferry from Marazion. Apart from the situation of this spectacular retreat, there is interest here for all. The harbour and village may always be visited, but visitors should check for opening days of the castle. In either case it would be easy to spend a whole day here thinking of the past: perhaps of 1497, when Perkin Warbeck left his wife on the Mount to make an abortive claim for England's throne; or of 1549, when the owners of the castle were involved in the Prayer Book Rebellion; possibly even of 1642-3 when the future King Charles II was given sanctuary *en route* for the Isles of Scilly.

In 1981 an unusual scheme was proposed by Lord St Levan. He decided to reconstruct a twelfth-century monastic herb garden. His idea was to grow medicinal plants used by the Benedictines — especially those for the relief of toothache, as they were much sought after by pilgrims. When the plan

reaches its final stages, this area of the Mount will add to the already considerable attractions of the place.

Marazion is usually interpreted 'Little Market', but probably 'Small Sea' is a better meaning of the unusual name: *mara* — sea and *zion* — from vyghan or small. The latter describes perfectly the narrow strip of water between the village and the Mount, which can perhaps be seen to better advantage from the higher villages inland.

Ludgvan (Lugian) is a quiet churchtown set well above the bay amidst narrow, twisting lanes. Dr William Borlase, born at Pendeen in 1695, was village rector for fifty-two years and published several books, including *The Natural History of Cornwall* in 1758, thirty-one years before Gilbert White's *History of Selborne*. This energetic clergyman was the first

St Ludgvan

archaeologist to detail the heritage of Beaker Age monuments, and his work in this field is still unsurpassed.

From the steep B3309 below the church towards Crowlas the second lane on the left leads to the exciting Penwith countryside that Borlase studied. A lane curves round the foot of Trencrom Hill — a National Trust area, ideal for views, walks and picnics. It consists of sixty-four acres of gorse-covered hill, overlooking an expanse of both land and sea. Here are numerous well-preserved antiquities — an Iron-Age stone-walled hill-fort enclosing several hut circles. Legend says that Giant Trecobben used to throw 'pebbles' at his brother Cormorran who lived on the Mount: the gigantic Bowl Rock beside the Lelant-Towednack road to the north, given to the Trust in 1962, has the notice 'thrown by a giant!' The café at the foot of the hill has leaflets about this interesting archaeological site.

Further along the same road is Trink — once reputed to be the home of another giant, but now a delightful place for holidaymakers. North-east from here a turning off the B3311 leads to lonely Towednack church.

The way to Castle-an-Dinas and Chysauster is down the Nancledra valley, where tin has been streamed since earliest times. The former is one of the chain of hill forts across the country, the latter (along a pleasant lane off the B3311) probably one of the best preserved beehive hut circles in Great Britain. It was an Iron Age village from about the second century BC to the third century AD, and consists now of a series of stone houses, each containing a number of rooms. Partial excavations have been made here, and the walls of the buildings are still clearly visible. Not far away is Mulfra Quoit, a close group of standing stones on the site of an

Trencrom

ancient settlement at Mulfra Hill, which gives substantial evidence of ancient ley lines.

Also in the same area is the Men-an-Tol, the Men Scryfa (Inscribed Stone) and the Nine Maidens Stone Circle. Were these stones really once girls who had danced on the Sabbath and been turned to stone for their sin? That is what the legend says. The Men Scryfa, however, is thought to be closer to reality — some think it was the grave of a giant warrior, others consider it another ley marker, and there are those who think it could be the gravestone of Rialobran (Royal Raven) who lived between the fifth and sixth centuries BC on nearby Carn Galver.

Beside the lonely secondary road which runs from Morvah to Madron stands Lanyon Quoit — probably Cornwall's most famous monument and the only known example of the remains of a long barrow. It was originally 90ft long and its capstone was so high that

Places of Interest North and East of Penzance

St Michael's Mount (National Trust)
Originally the site of a Benedictine chapel established by Edward the Confessor.

Trencrom SW 518362 (National Trust)
Between St Michael's Mount and St Ives, this hill fort has fine views over Cornwall's narrowest part.

Chysauster
2½m north-west of Gulval
An Iron Age village dating from the second century BC to the third century AD. Interesting series of stone houses, each with rooms.

Mulfra Quoit
At head of Trevaylor Valley, this monument towers over Penwith with three of four uprights standing.

Men-Scryfa
3m north-west of Madron
Up a side lane beside the Morvah to Madron road is an 8ft tall inscribed stone.

Men-an-Tol
A fascinating monument, with numerous legends, but few facts. In 1749 Dr Borlase learnt that local people still crept through the hole to cure their rheumatism and local children suffering from rickets were passed through it at certain times of the year.

Lanyon Quoit (National Trust)
4m north-west of Penzance
A huge granite capstone on three upright stones, Cornwall's most famous antiquity, and the most restored.

Madron Well and Baptistry B3212
Water from here said to have effected many miraculous cures. Baptistry restored.

Trengwainton Gardens A3071
(National Trust)
Beautiful gardens full of exotic plants in springtime.

Dr Borlase rode his horse under it. Storm damage accounts for the present lower height.

Madron village is where this road joins the B3312 into Penzance. It is high over the port and has a huddle of cottages pleasantly grouped near the church, which is named after a sixth-century holy man from Brittany, Maddern. It is the mother church of Penzance and, acknowledged to be one of Cornwall's finest, is well worth a visit. The pew ends are unusually fine; here are the Nelson banner (mentioned earlier) and the great bell from the famous Ding-Dong mine, whose ruined engine-house is silhouetted starkly on the high land ridge behind the village. A short distance away is Madron's famous Wishing Well, and those who care to walk about half a mile down a damp ferny lane will probably see rags hanging from the surrounding bushes which are still offered to St Maddern, possibly for happiness in love, or simply to placate the invisible spirits and hope for their protection.

The lovely Trengwainton Gardens, a National Trust property, lie beside the A3071 below Madron. There has been a house here since the sixteenth century, but it is now privately owned by Major Simon Bolitho. In 1814, Rose Price, the son of a rich West Indian sugar planter

Lanyon Quoit

bought the house and estate and began to develop it along the lines seen today. He enlarged the original house, gave it a granite facade, built the lodge, created the walled gardens and planted the magnificent woods of beech and sycamore which are so admired today. The walled gardens contain many tender plants which cannot be grown in the open anywhere else in England, and although Trengwainton is always lovely, it is at its best in the spring.

Brenda Wootton, Cornwall's popular folk singer, has a song called *My Yesterday Town*. It is about Newlyn, where she was born, and she looks back sadly to former times when it was an important fishing harbour, before artists and visitors poured in to intrude on the intimacy of its community life. Then it was a village with five bridges, five pubs, one church and cottages tip-tilting down the hill to the sea, their livelihood, their joy and their sorrow. Memories of sadness are still retained in the name Mount Misery, high above the bay. This was where anxious wives and sweethearts watched during storms, fearful that their men might not return.

The fisherman's world is no longer the same, but the charm of the old cottages remains, and still there is the fine quality of clear light which later on attracted Stanhope Forbes and other artists who exhibited in the Newlyn Art Gallery at the turn of the twentieth century.

The name Penlee reverberated round the land like the tolling of a funeral bell at the end of 1981 when storms off this coast caused a lifeboat tragedy. Penlee Point is on the coast road to Mousehole (Mouzel), the prettiest fishing village according to many visitors, and which, with Penzance and Newlyn, was burned and almost destroyed by the Spaniards in July 1595. Its delightful cluster of cottages hugging the harbour appeals to artists, photographers and most holiday-makers. Others enjoy visiting the Bird Hospital on Raginnis Hill — founded by the Yglesias sisters, but now under the auspices of the RSPCA.

Only two miles along the cliff path, but further by road past the Roman encampment of Castallack, lies the fertile and lovely Lamorna valley. A bubbling trout stream and colourful gardens tempt visitors down to the little harbour, enticing them to linger. The artist Lamorna Birch could not leave, and even used the local name for his paintings: perhaps it would not have been quite so well-known, had it not been for his decision to stay and paint.

The ten-mile cliff walk from here to Land's End is one that should not be hurried. There are flowers, birds and views sufficient to satisfy everyone, but few know the story of how the famous Marconi met and fell in love with Betty Paynter on the Lamorna cliffs. She was then the fifteen-year-old daughter of Colonel Paynter of nearby Boskenna House, but the vast difference in age did not stop the engineer. He installed a radio receiver in her schoolroom at home, sent diamond bracelets to her at school and sailed his yacht into Bournemouth almost every weekend in the hope of a meeting. A story in the best romantic tradition, but one that did not end according to the Cinderella pattern. After three years of fun and friendship, the schoolgirl, then grown up, realised that the love was all on his side and refused him — not for the first time, but the last.

Above Lamorna Cove, past Trewoofe (Troove), is Boleigh, site of the last battle between the Cornish and the English, which took place in AD 935. To celebrate his victory, King Athelstan gave a charter to found a collegiate church at St Buryan. The two immense megaliths known as The Pipers are believed to have been erected by the king as peace stones to seal the treaty. On the other side of the road is another group of stones — the Merry Maidens (Heath of Mordred). It consists of nineteen stones, is about 75ft in diameter, and is one of the places where the Cornish Gorsedd is sometimes held.

St Buryan is a handsome church of the late fifteenth century with a fine rood screen and a 92ft granite tower. Further along the B3283, lies the village of Treen, once a busy tin-streaming area, now only seen as a lovely wooded valley leading to the National Trust properties of Penberth Cove and part of Treryn Dinas. The cove is a reminder, perhaps, of the way of life once common in many Cornish fishing communities where wives and children grew violets and narcissi for the London market. This trade developed considerably after the opening of Brunel's Royal Albert Bridge in 1859. Since the property passed to the Trust in 1957, many of the small gardens are still cultivated, and inshore fishermen are as active as their forefathers in previous centuries.

Places of Interest West of Penzance

Newlyn Art Gallery
24 New Road
Donated to artists and the community in 1895 by Passmore Edwards.

Mousehole Bird Hospital
Opened as a bird sanctuary in 1928. Now run by RSPCA.

Merry Maidens B3315
Best-known stone circle stands in meadow and is sometimes the site for the Cornish Gorsedd.

Treryn Dinas
Porthcurno
198 acres of land owned by the National Trust in the Porthcurno coastal area, including the Iron Age fort of Treryn Dinas..

Minack Theatre
Porthcurno
A unique open-air theatre fashioned from natural rock amphitheatre.

Chapel Carn Brea
Near Land's End
Covers fifty-three acres and is England's 'first and last' hill. Mediaeval chapel remains on summit.

Carn Euny Ancient Village
Sancreed
A notable Iron Age village, having a 60ft fougou.

Drift Reservoir
Pleasant for walks and picnics.

The fine jagged headland of Treryn (Treen) Dinas forms one side of Porthcurno, a bay of startling blues and greens with the Minack Open-Air Theatre on its other side. Treryn Fort, of thirty-six acres, incorporates a complex of defensive ditches dating from the Iron Age. Here is the famous Logan Rock, once moved ill-advisedly by Oliver Goldsmith's nephew for a prank. It weighs 66 tons, and the over-enthusiastic young man had to replace it at his own expense. As space is limited on this headland, visitors must leave their cars above the bridge over the stream and walk the last quarter of a mile.

Motorists who leave the B3315 to drive to Porthcurno Beach and on to the Minack Theatre must be prepared for narrow and winding lanes. The road passes the Cable and Wireless training school before the car park nearest to the beach. Theatregoers have to drive up the steep road beyond to reach their destination, but this unique place should not be missed. In 1932, Miss Rowena Cade and her gardener began the amazing task of creating an amphitheatre out of the natural rock on the cliff edge. Stone seats now replace the grassy ledges, sound and lighting and dressing-room accommodation are of the best, but the original magic remains. No matter what the play or the players, the setting makes every performance one of individual delight — the sight of the moon rising over the backcloth of ocean is a never-to-be-forgotten experience.

The church of St Levan and its holy well lies beyond the Minack; as the road stops there, motorists must return to the B3315 for Land's End. The walk along the coast from here takes about two and a half hours. On a fine day the views are unrivalled and even Humphry Davy was inspired to write poetry about them when he walked there in stormy weather.

In 1982 David Goldstone bought this part of the nation's heritage and made it known that his plans were to make the fullest use of its natural resources while conserving its dramatic beauty. This is

another place for a whole day's exploration; photographers, botanists, poets and holidaymakers of all ages will find something here to please them. Longships lighthouse lies due west of the last group of rocks while seven or eight miles beyond is Wolf Rock. This was the place used by Trinity House for their successful experiments in airlifting supplies to lighthouse crews, many of whom now enjoy the benefit of food and mail delivered on time, as well as being able to leave when their spell of duty has finished.

About a mile to the north lies Sennen, near the Mayon and Trevescan Cliffs, both National Trust properties. The former has on it a good example of a Cornish cliff castle (Mayon meaning Maen or Stone) with sheer drops to the sea and a view of basking sharks cruising off the rocks in summer. Above Sennen Cove, which continues on to Whitesand Bay, is the ancient church of St Sennen, the westernmost church in England. It is small and low, as befits its site and was re-consecrated in 1440.

Before the village of Crows-an-Wra (Witch's Cross) several paths leave the main road and climb to Chapel Carn Brea, which also belongs to the National Trust. It is the first and last hill in England, and is reputed to have the widest sea view visible from the mainland of the British Isles. Two Bronze Age barrows and the remains of a mediaeval chapel dedicated to St Michael may be seen at the end of the gentle climb to the top, where in 1907 one of Cornwall's largest Bronze Age urns (now in the Truro Museum) was found. Today at this place, members of the St Just Old Cornwall Society light the first in the chain of forty bonfires which illuminate Cornwall on Midsummer Eve from Land's End to the Tamar. This is an interesting and festive occasion. Songs and prayers (often in Cornish) accompany the 'sacrifice' of herbs and flowers thrown in the flames by the Lady of the Flowers to propitiate the sun god. In other words — a plea shared by all visitors — for summer sunshine.

The whole area is good for picnics and walks, and for exploring the nearby antiquities. Carn Euny is an ancient Iron Age village now cared for by the Department of the Environment. The remains are said to rival those of Chysauster and there is the added attraction of a fine 60ft-long fougou, or underground chamber. The Blind Fiddler Stone — source of many legends — stands beside the A30, and down a farm lane opposite is Boscawen-noon, an isolated stone circle with a central heel stone or altar. Henry Jenner, who revived the Cornish Gorsedd in 1928, chose this place for its first assembly.

Nearby Sancreed church is worth looking at. There is a good rood screen, original barrel roofing and five crosses in the churchyard. One which has lilies on it is noteworthy. Half hidden in trees in a nearby field is the Sancreed holy well and baptistry possessing an exceptional air of mystery and sanctity.

The road runs past Drift Reservoir to join the A30, but old mingles with new here, for Drift village is mentioned in Cornwall's best-known folk tale — John of Chyannor. He left Treen when mining was at a low ebb and went to look for work in the east. That to him was not land overseas but a farm a few miles east of Marazion. This particular story is especially interesting, as it names all the places John visited in his wandering — something which does not often occur in folk tales. Deep in the valley of Buryas Bridge there is a cross inscribed with symbols of the Cretan mysteries — another link with the strange past of West Penwith.

To see the best of the northern part of this peninsula follow the A3071 out of Penzance. It passes Castle Horneck shortly after leaving the edge of the town — a splendid place for a Youth Hostel, as it was once the home of the Levelis or Lovell family. They owned much of the land in this area in early mediaeval times and were greatly involved in the Crusades.

The countryside around St Just is almost other-worldly; its small fields and dry stone walls bring to mind the first men who settled here many centuries ago. The tower of the church, though low, can be seen from quite a distance, as it has stood in granite solidity since the fifteenth century. Near the clock tower a grassy arena is used today for the ceremony of choosing the Carnival Queen. It is in fact a plain-an-gwary, for performances of mediaeval miracle plays.

Cape Cornwall Street leads to Great Britain's only cape, ideal for walks, picnics and birdwatching in fine weather. Seals are sometimes seen off shore in the summer. The picturesque nineteenth-century ventilator shaft at the summit is a reminder of the many mines which once operated here. Beyond Land's End is the Longships lighthouse but in the other direction are the picturesque ruins of the Crowns section of the Botallack Mine. The Prince and Princess of Wales (later King Edward VII and Queen Alexandra) came here in 1865, descending the mine in 'special' clothes which today would certainly not be permitted.

Tunnels 7ft by 4ft were cut into a rich copper lode under the sea bed eventually reaching 1,360ft below sea level nearly half a mile from shore, and men worked there each day. When the quarterly accounts were produced, mine managers

Porth Ledden and Cape Cornwall

and owners would celebrate their gains with a feast at the Count House — now a restaurant.

The coastal path goes along these cliffs, skirting the village of Trewellard with its plain, bleak church built by the miners in 1851 to their parson's design. Behind it lies Chun Castle, a magnificent hill fort built before 200BC. A short distance away stands the much older Chun Cromlech. Pendeen Manor, a sixteenth-century farm was the birthplace of Dr Borlase, father of Cornish archaeology. In the yard there is a fogou or underground passage which runs in one direction for 23ft and in another for 33ft. At the angle of one of these is another chamber — a foot longer than the first passage. There has been much speculation as to the original use of these constructions — there are a

number of them in Cornwall. Archaeologists have not yet produced a satisfactory reason for their existence; so no-one knows whether fogous were built for storage, defence or primitive housing.

Past the manor, the road leads to Pendeen Watch — a lighthouse open every day except Sunday. Perched on a cliff edge, it is surrounded by open land where there are birds and flowers in plenty. Here, too, at Pendeen, beside the B3306 is Geevor Tin Mine, a thriving Cornish industry in a spectacular cliff setting. It was registered as a limited company in 1911, based on the old mines of Wheal Stennack and the ill-fated Levant. Tin and copper were mined from its rich workings until disaster struck in 1919. The man-engine, carrying its full complement of men to

Day's end at St Austell

Polperro

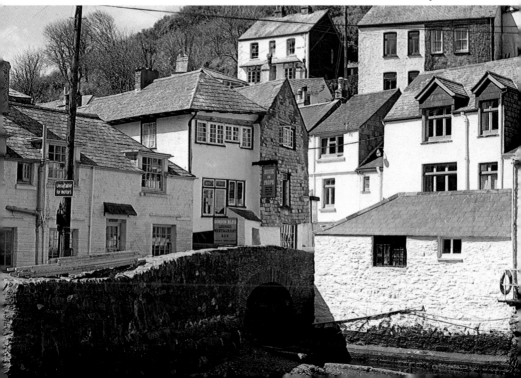

Veryan round house

the surface, broke, crashed in ruins down the shaft and killed thirty-one miners. The deeper workings were then abandoned and from 1930 work there ceased altogether, until modern machinery was installed in Geevor. Today this is the only mine working in an area which supported about twenty in 1870. Some of their ruins, still picturesque, though sad, stand along the cliffs, slowly but surely weathering away.

It is good, however, to look at the progress made at Geevor since 1919, when work was started on a new shaft. In 1965 the Boscaswell Downs Mine was included in the workings. Altogether they now extend for more than two square miles under the Atlantic and include the Levant area which was so rich in tin and copper during the middle of the nineteenth century. Geevor Mine has already reached a depth of over 2,000ft and part of the plans for its future concerns further development under the ocean. Visitors are taken on guided tours of the working treatment plant which produces the tin concentrate; a mining museum is there for those who wish to learn more. Plenty of parking space is available — well-sited and made pleasant for those who like to picnic.

In Boscaswell village is Pendeen Crafts with its adjoining small museum of mining memorabilia. The outstanding feature of this display is a nine-foot high model of Botallack Mine in its heyday, made by Clive Carter, a local mining engineer. It is a scenic arrangement showing the cliffside Crowns enginehouse and the celebrated Boscawen Diagonal Shaft visited by the Prince and Princess of Wales in 1865.

The area from here to Zennor is particularly interesting, especially at

The Crowns, Botallack

Bosigran, beyond Morvah, on the National Trust cliffs. These are wild and exposed, but man has learnt how to survive here from pre-historic times, sheltering his crops and animals in tiny fields surrounded by their stone hedges which remain from the Iron Age. The adventurous will probably enjoy the circular walk westwards from Porthmeor Cove to Bosigran Castle, along the spur path past the Climbers' Club hut, and back to Porthmeor Cove along the main road. Adjoining Bosigran is more National Trust property, with a rather special history. It was here during World War II that commandos trained — the western side of the valley is in fact named 'Commando Ridge'. Here, too, Lord John Hunt and Sherpa Tensing climbed together to celebrate the tenth anniversary of the ascent of Everest. Never before had Tensing seen the sea and it was his first experience of cliff climbing. Cars can be parked by the road, and access to the coast is by the spur path previously mentioned.

The village of Porthmeor is missed by

Places of Interest Northwest of Penzance

Chun Castle and Cromlech
1m from Morvah
Both antiquities are important, the castle being an outstanding hill fort, the only one of stone in Cornwall.

Pendeen Lighthouse
Built by Trinity House in 1900. Its warning light gives four white flashes every second, while its fog signal blasts seven seconds every minute.

Geevor Mine Museum B3306
in Pendeen village
This mine has been operating since 1911 and is still in full production. It offers an insight into present-day mining techniques. History of the industry can also be seen here. Underground workings now extend for more than two square miles, and mainly under the Atlantic, and include Levant Mine. In the last century, Levant was one of the most successful in the area, working tin and copper.
The unusual name of this mine comes from *gever* the plural of *gavar* (goat in Cornish) — very suitable here as the gorse-covered cliffs once supported many of these creatures.

St Just Plain-an-Gwarry
An open, grassy area used until 1600 for mediaeval miracle plays. Gorsedd sometimes held here.

Botallack
Romantic ruins on the lower cliffs below the Count House are the Crowns section of this mine.

Pendeen Crafts and Mining Museum
Boscaswell village
In this small local collection relevant to mining is a scenic model of the spectacular cliffside Crowns enginehouse and the Boscawen Diagonal Shaft which lead to the undersea levels of Botallack Mine. This nine-foot high representation recalls the mine in its heyday and when the Prince and Princess of Wales visited it in 1865. It is the work of Clive Carter, a mining engineer who lives in the West Penwith area.

Wayside Museum
Zennor
On the St Ives to Land's End coastal road the exhibits of this privately owned museum include tools and implements connected with the mining, agricultural, quarrying and domestic life of Zennor.

most people who, not unnaturally, are eager to reach Zennor. It is, however, worth asking at Borthpennis for permission to cross the private land and look at the Iron Age village courtyard house. It is similar in many respects to Chysauster, but, in addition, has its own fortification and gatehouse, and is one of the best of the numerous ancient monuments scattered on the downs above the B3306.

Today Zennor is a picturesque miniature village lying in the slight shelter of Trewey Hill. It has, however, a long and interesting history. Isolated as it was by the natural features of land and sea, Zennor remained almost inaccessible for centuries — which is why the presence of the past is still so strong in and around it. The small fields of Middle and Late Bronze -Age settlements are still to be seen at Trewey and Wicca. Some tools and farm implements used for agricultural work down the years are among the exhibits in the small Wayside Museum, close to the car park. Whether mining is quite as old as farming here no-one knows, but it is said that tin-streaming has thoroughly worked almost every area of the Foage valley (Zennor river). Tools used for this are another feature of the museum. Both these industries were quite local, but Zennor's stone-workers were once famous beyond their homes. Tradition tells that the granite for St Ives' Church was brought by sea from here — boats sometimes having to wait for weeks in order to take advantage of a spell of rare fine weather. Great cubes of Zennor rock were also used in the construction of Falmouth harbour, and some went to London for pavement edging.

The square church tower is not high, but it stands as a clear marker of the centre of Zennor life. On the outside wall of the church just inside the gate is

Zennor mermaid

John Davey's memorial stone: A man of history, said to have been the last one to speak traditional Cornish. There are only two old bench ends in the church, but one of them, unusually interesting, portrays a finely carved mermaid, and recalls the story of the beautiful sea-creature whose charms were the downfall of Matthew Trewhella. Opposite is the Tinner's Arms — so old that its origins are unknown.

Behind the inn the path which runs parallel to a trout stream flowing into Pendour (Mermaid) Cove leads down to Zennor Head. This is part of the eighty-four acres owned by the National Trust along the cliff, enabling walkers to enjoy the delights of thyme-scented springy turf all the way to Wicca Pool.

The quickest way back to Penzance is up Trewey Hill and over the moor.

6 The Isles of Scilly

The Scillies consist of more than three hundred islands; but only six are inhabited. These are St Mary's, Tresco, St Martin's, St Agnes, Bryher and Gugh, their total acreage being only 4,400. St Agnes, though almost the smallest, has the special distinction of being the most southerly inhabited point in Great

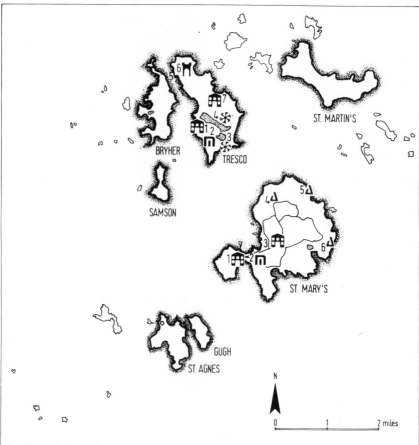

ST. MARY'S : 1. Garrison. 2. Museum. 3. Harry's Walls. 4. Bants Carn. 5. Innisidgen Carn. 6. Porth Hellick Down.
TRESCO : 1. Abbey Gardens. 2. Valhalla. 3. Abbey Pool. 4. Great Pool. 5. Cromwell's Castle. 6. King Charles's Castle. 7. Block House.

CHAPTER 6

Britain. Situated about twenty-six miles west of Land's End, they are unique in their relationship to the mainland. Though associated with Cornwall, they are not part of it, as any true Scillonian will stoutly maintain. Nor do they belong to England, in spite of a recent imposition of taxes that makes them technically so.

For a considerable saving of time, most visitors prefer to travel by air, either from Penzance or Newquay. Though it can be extremely rough even in summer, others enjoy the $2^1/_2$ hour sea journey in *Scillonian III*, launched by Prince Charles in 1977. The first sight of the islands almost contradicts the various names given to them over the centuries — Isles of the Blest, Paradise Islands and the Lotus Isles. The immediate impression is of rocky outcrops with scarcely any trees. But soon the unusual peace and quiet — part of Scilly's charm — takes over and the almost complete absence of vehicles makes itself felt. As a result visitors are still able to enjoy startling blue seas, silver sands on empty beaches, birds and flowers that are different, as well as a stone 'library' of instant pre-history consisting of more than one hundred and fifty Bronze Age relics. That the islands have maintained their reputation as a lifeline to tranquillity is largely the result of careful administration by its owners, the Duchy of Cornwall, and their tenants, the Island Council, who have prevented any development that

Sunrise over St Mary's

might spoil the Scillies' unique beauty.

Unlike anywhere else in the British Isles, Scilly, with its exceptionally soft climate, is the ideal place for open-air holiday-makers in late February or early March. This is the time when the flower harvest is at its height and the fields of floral 'sunshine' rival even the brilliance of the sun. The atmosphere is different from that of the summer season and visitors enjoy being part of the concentration on flower exporting which pervades the islands in early spring. The flower show which takes place in March is no ordinary show, but is the oldest in the country, because Scillonian growers were among the first in Britain to develop the flower industry. It began here in a very strange manner, when William Trevillick, who farmed on Rocky Hill, St Mary's, packed a few blooms in his Aunt Ellen's hatbox and sent them as an experiment to Covent Garden Market. The date of that inspiration is thought to be as early as 1867, but it makes little difference. What is important is that it came at a time when the islanders were desperate for a new source of income.

Kelp-making, which ended with the introduction of synthetic iodine in 1835, was superseded by boat-building. But this ended about 1870 when sail gave way to steam; so the industry resulting from Trevillick's brain child was eagerly welcomed. It was encouraged by Augustus Smith, who also fostered the potato trade and introduced Guernsey cattle to the farmers. His enthusiasm and foresight undoubtedly saved the Isles of Scilly from the fate suffered by some Scottish islands, whose inhabitants were forced to leave for lack of employment. But the flower growing, too, is now in decline, although many of the fields are still golden in spring. Today's industry is tourism.

Places of Interest on St Mary's

The Garrison and Star Castle
Garrison Gate was built in 1742 as part of the garrison wall extending round the promontory. Today there are batteries, a park and promenade. Star Castle was a fortress erected by Elizabeth I and has walls projecting at eight salient angles. The inner building had two upper storeys and a bellcote. 18ft thick ramparts and a dry moat surround it. Since 1933 it has been an hotel; the dungeons are now a bar.

Museum
Church Steet, Hugh Town
Built in 1967, it displays all facets of past and present life on the islands.

Porth Hellick Down
The beach is rich in seashells. Sir Cloudesley Shovel's monument is at the eastern end of the bay, also an hill fort and the rock formation called the Loaded Camel. Nearby is a burial chamber.

Harry's Walls
Begun about fifty years before Star Castle. Originally square with four bastions.

Bant's Carn
This burial chamber was probably built about 2,000BC. It remained in use for five hundred years.

Innisidgen Carn
There are two monuments — upper and lower. The former is a mound about 26ft diameter.

St Mary's is the main island. Hugh Town, the rather splendid name for its 'capital', is built on the isthmus which separates The Garrison area from the main part. It is here that many visitors stay when they arrive either at the airport terminal near Old Town or at the harbour of Hugh Town. In this small capital there are numerous shops, two banks, the main post office, and three churches of different denominations. The Town Hall serves a dual purpose, as performances of concerts and plays are held here during the season. The Island Museum, opened only in 1967, has interesting displays which cover the archaeology, wild life and history of Scilly. Its central feature is a fully-rigged pilot gig (a Scillonian speciality) and there is also an appropriate number of wreck relics.

Naturally, there is a considerable amount of boating and fishing here, and from St Mary's Quay, the popular sport of gig-racing can be watched and enjoyed every week during the summer. These unique craft, some over a hundred years old, are built to a special island design. They were originally used by local pilots, who raced their boats out into the Channel, each one hoping to be the first aboard sailing ships needing guidance through the dangerous coastal waters. The gigs were doubtless put to other uses as well, for their slim lines gave them the extra speed necessary to escape officials on the lookout for smugglers.

St Mary's Quay is also the point of departure for inter-island boat trips: these are particularly delightful in the spring when the seabird sanctuaries can be seen at close quarters. (The Island of Annet is closed to all visitors from 15 April to 20 August to protect the nesting birds.) Atlantic grey seals can also be seen easily from these inter-island launches. Some of them take visitors out as far as Bishop Rock Lighthouse, seven miles to the west; the more fortunate will be able to see the relief by helicopter of the lighthouse keepers. It is easy to understand why some visitors consider these boat trips to be the highlight of their holiday.

Perhaps one of the greatest attractions of the Isles of Scilly is the seclusion of its sandy beaches. They are all safe for bathing, and even in high summer remain uncrowded. There are, however, two danger spots. The sand bars connecting St Mary's with Toll's Island and St Agnes with Gugh are unsafe when the water flows over the two bars, but that is only at high tide. The clear waters attract skindivers particularly, on account of the marine life and the numerous wrecks. The authorities, who know the swell conditions and tidal streams, recommend divers to operate in groups under supervision, particularly as the nearest decompression chamber is at Plymouth, some 120 miles away.

If the weather is right, visitors usually take a short circular walk around the Garrison walls on their first evening as the fine sunsets over Samson are not to be missed. This is when one begins to appreciate the wisdom of the local Council ruling: 'Caravans, motorised caravans and similar vehicles MAY NOT be brought to the islands. PRIVATE CARS ARE MOST UNWELCOME AND ARE QUITE UNNECESSARY FOR THE ENJOYMENT OF A HOLIDAY IN THE ISLANDS (there are approximately nine miles of road on St Mary's).' Taxis and bus services cater for all necessary transport.

Garrison Gate was not built until 1742, although Star Castle, (an hotel since 1933) was constructed in 1593 at the top of the hill, as a defence against possible Spanish attack. The population then moved from Old Town to greater safety near the castle.

There is a coastal path here, as elsewhere on the island, but another leads straight down to Woolpack Point where two rusty old cannons still point seawards, as if awaiting the enemy.

Sir Cloudesley Shovel's monument and 'loaded Camel'

From here, if the weather is good, there is a fine view across St Mary's Sound to the islands of St Agnes and Gugh, but it is a place to avoid during a north-westerly gale. Returning to Hugh Town, the road passes The Duchy of Cornwall's Land Steward's impressive granite offices. They overlook Porth Cressa, St Mary's central and most popular beach.

The exploration of the main part of the island begins at Peninnis Head. The shorter way leads to the church, begun by King William IV and finished in 1837 by Augustus Smith. Past the vicarage is the island power station, skilfully built in an old quarry, and at the top of the hill is Buzza Tower. This was constructed in 1821 as an old Spanish-style windmill to grind corn; after which it was converted into a tower to commemorate King Edward VII's visit in 1902. It now has an even more useful role as a landmark for shipping. A bumpy track between a granite-walled

lane leads eventually to Peninnis Head, a magnificent, rugged promontory at this southern extremity of St Mary's. Here even the granite has been smoothed and weathered by storms; the resulting shapes deserve names such as the Tuskless Elephant, the Toastrack, and the Kettle and Pans, (where shrimps are plentiful).

The path to Old Town and its bay passes the mediaeval church, now only fragmentary remains of a once large cruciform building. The churchyard is full of memorials to Scillonians and other seamen wrecked off this coast. Some of the men were from Sir Cloudesley Shovel's ill-fated fleet, notably Henry Trelawny, son of the famous Bishop from Pelynt, near Looe, captain of one of the ships. Here, too, victims of the HMS *Schiller* disaster in 1851 are buried. A memorial for those who died in both World Wars and a monument to Augustus Smith are also to be found in the cemetery.

Pelistry Bay, St Mary's

From Hugh Town the road goes past the lifeboat slips and turns right at Parting Carn for Porth Hellick. The coastal path also reaches this point too. Here is the quartz monument to Sir Cloudesley Shovel whose flagship *Association* was wrecked in 1707, the most valuable underwater treasure ever located round the British Isles, discovered in 1967. Since then the *Romney, Eagle* and *Firebrand* have been found, the last-named as recently as 1981. The Admiral's personal plate alone would be worth a small fortune today, but the hazardous diving conditions have clearly hindered rescue operations, although the divers still persevere.

On these downs is a group of five chambered tombs, all very close together. Most of these 4,000-year-old passage graves are crumbling; the best preserved is maintained by the Department of the Environment.

The coastal path carries on to Pelistry Bay where the sand is especially beautiful (felspar and quartz) and the sea views hard to beat. This is where swimmers need to avoid bathing when the sea covers the bar. Inland is Holy Vale, believed to have been the site of either a convent or a monastic cell, and the path continues to picturesque Watermill Bay, past coastal indentations, before returning to Hugh Town.

Telegraph Walk, as it is called, starts at the lifeboat slips, and goes to Porth

Places of Interest on Tresco

Abbey Gardens
A delightful place where an immense variety of plants is grown. By the old pump the Pump Garden leads to the ruins of the old priory, inside which are graves dating from the Dissolution of 1539 to 1820. There is also a small stone under the archway which suggests that it was a Christian tombstone of the fifth or sixth century AD. Pebble Gardens, Neptune's Steps and terraces are other delights from the many in the Tresco Abbey Gardens.

Abbey Pool and Great Pool
Two lakes populated with geese and ducks, popular with birdlovers.

Valhalla
A museum for the preservation of carved, wooden figure-heads from over seventy ships wrecked off the islands.

Cromwell's Castle
It was built in 1651 by Admiral Blake of the Republican forces and consists of a 60ft circular tower and granite platform to command the channel between Bryher and Tresco.

King Charles' Castle
This earthwork is of similar design to others in the period. A pentagonal fort was added in the Civil War.

The Old Blockhouse
This was built towards the end of the sixteenth century as an artillery battery. It is above Old Grimsby.

Tresco Abbey gardens

Cromwell's Castle, Tresco

Mellon and Porth Harry. Here are the uncompleted sixteenth-century fortifications known as Harry's Walls. Visitors can enjoy the facilities of the golf course beyond Porthloo Beach, but coastguards at Telegraph Tower are always on watch, and send meteorological readings to the London Air Ministry for weather forecasting. On the rough cliff slopes, near Bant's Carn, is another of the Department of the Environment's properties — a burial chamber and village of the Roman period.

At the pine-fringed northern tip of St Mary's lies Bar Point where there is some of the best bathing. Here, are two more Department of the Environment monuments — the Innisidgen prehistoric burial chambers.

Before leaving St Mary's, Scilly's main island, there is an interesting point to consider about the western lighthouses. Eight of them can be seen from here on a clear night. Bishop Rock, Peninnis Head, Sevenstones and Round Island are in the locality. Farther away are Wolf Rock and Longships off Land's End, while on Cornwall's mainland Pendeen and the Lizard are also visible.

Tresco's 735 acres might well be considered a complete nature reserve, the population living mainly in a line of hamlets across the central neck of the area. It differs from the other islands as it is leased privately from the Duchy. There are no cars, caravans or motor cycles — nor is camping allowed. The beauty of this place, and probably the conservation of the entire group, is due to the vision of Augustus Smith. In 1834 he became Lord Protector of Scilly, and lived first on Tresco, before emigrating to St Mary's. This extraordinary man with the very ordinary name was a far-sighted visionary from Hereford who gave the islands new life, simply by rooting out the cause of their deterioration — an ancient system of land tenure.

This had resulted in serious unemployment caused by a surplus population; so he put the men to work building roads and the wall boundaries which were the beginning of the famous Tresco Abbey botanical gardens. Smith created them on the site of a tenth-century Benedictine Abbey and, in the equable climate and natural shelter, made the barren island blossom with sub-tropical plants sheltered by Californian and Monterey pines.

South from Timothy's Corner at New Grimsby, the path leads past the Bulb Farm (picking starts here before Christmas) and skirts Appletree Bay. At low water it is possible to walk across the flats to Samson — though speed is essential to avoid being cut off.

Inland lies the Great Pool, which, with the smaller Abbey Pool, occupies about forty-six acres. A great concentration of bird life on these waters attracts bird-lovers, who come especially to see the rare migrants that breed here. About fifty species nest in the island and probably more are seen here than anywhere else in Europe.

Through the beauty of Abbey Wood there is a way to the Abbey Gardens themselves. It is impossible to describe such a place briefly, for it is unique. But there are more than five thousand species of plants from a hundred countries and from every climatic region in the world — many brought by Scillonian seamen returning home from their voyages.

Yet within this paradise is another — the Valhalla Gardens. It is an appropriate name for the collection of figureheads and other relics washed ashore from over seventy ships wrecked in the area. It is a strange, eerie place, but it should not be overlooked.

The northern part of Tresco has cliff walks on heather, ling and short springy grass which lead to Cromwell's Castle. This substantially built round tower with its 12ft thick walls was erected in 1651 as a defence against the Dutch. There is King Charles' Castle, too; a long, low, oblong fort but so badly sited that the guns could not operate. Castle Downs has early tin-workings, and on the headland at Piper's Hole there is evidence of three more. Intrepid and agile visitors may scramble down this gully and find a large freshwater lake about 20yd by 4yd. Candlelight turns this unexpected discovery into a miniature fairyland, but it is only for experienced climbers. Old Blockhouse is nearby.

Samson consists only of two hills joined by an isthmus. It has become famous as the setting Sir Walter Besant used in his novel *Armorel of Lyonesse*. There is also a kistvaen or burial chamber here.

Bryher has been called 'the pearl of Scilly', but it is wild and untamed — lovely views but little else. People visit the outer islands for bird-watching — St Agnes, Gugh and Annet, a bird sanctuary.

7 The North Coast

Legends cannot be avoided in telling the story of Cornwall: that connected with St Ives has puzzled many people. It is said that the holy St Ia, the first to visit this part of the coast, did so on a leaf. Impossible today? But the re-enacted journey of St Brendan was made in a small boat covered with hide that might well have looked like a leaf. Nevertheless, St Ia did arrive and founded a settlement here which later became the busy and attractive fishing port of St Ives. Miraculous leaves are in short supply today: most visitors leave their cars at Lelant Saltings if they are on a day's outing. This avoids parking problems in the town and adds another pleasure, for if the weather is fine, there can be fewer delightful railway journeys than the one on the local train which runs from St Erth to St Ives and collects passengers on the way. It takes a little over ten minutes but covers what must be one of the country's loveliest coastal routes. From Lelant Saltings, with its bird hide and flat fascinating scenery, the train windows give extensive views along the famous five miles of golden sands from St Ives to Godrevy Point. There is only restricted vehicular access to the town during the season, and buses are available from the Trenwith car park on the outskirts but the train ride from Lelant is the ideal way to arrive at St Ives.

The steep, winding cobbled streets of this 'picturesque seaside town par excellence', as it has been called, do much to retain its Cornishness. Looking over the water at Westcott's Quay where The Warren turns into Pednolva Walk,

it is easy to understand why the St Ives Art Club decided to hold meetings in that wharfside fishing cellar. Turner was probably the first artist to visit and paint scenes of the town. That was in 1811, but it was Whistler and Sickert who, in 1884, actually established the art colony there. Later, in 1927, another group formed the Society of Artists — this was wider-ranging and included people like Sir Alfred Munnings, Lamorna Birch, Barbara Hepworth and Bernard Leach. In 1920 the now famous potter established a workshop at Higher Stennack on the B3306. It is still there and examples of his art are always on display. Stennack is from 'sten' (Cornish for 'tin') and the whole valley was once a profitable mining area. Wheal Trenwith was probably the most notable of the workings as it produced tin, copper, pitchblends and the radium used by Marie Curie in her experiments.

Barbara Hepworth lived and worked nearer the harbour behind the parish church. Many of her sculptures and paintings are now on permanent exhibition; the Tate Gallery bought her studio and garden and now administers the museum.

In 1977 five people decided to hold an Arts Festival in St Ives — it was to be a local event marking the end of the summer season. It has, however, proved so popular that it has become a limited company covering every branch of the arts, and aims to encourage all artists. It now needs two weeks to cover its numerous activities, always beginning on the first Saturday of September.

The famous huer's hut on The Island

beside St Nicholas' Chapel looks down on the harbour and Smeaton's Pier. In former days, the look-out would watch for pilchards and cry 'Hevva' to the waiting fishermen. After a good catch, the toast would be the one now sadly outdated, of 'Fish, Tin and Copper'. Those times have certainly gone, but the nearby St Ives Museum has a fine collection of exhibits which vividly recall the past.

One of them, however, is certainly not maritime but is a reminder of St Ives' famous cat population. The rhyme 'As I was going to St Ives. . .' is well known to youngsters who use fingers and toes to count the 'kits, cats, sacks and wives'. Whether these words refer to this town or not, there remains no doubt that two

special types of cat are particularly associated with it. One is short-backed and stubby-legged, the other a large, contented animal resembling Alice in Wonderland's Cheshire cat. However, the animal traps on show in the museum — one displaying three mice, indicate that the cats enjoyed local fish and would certainly not bother to chase and catch mice.

A large part of the main room is devoted to material about John Knill (1733 - 1811), perhaps the most memorable of all St Ives' citizens. Customs officer, mayor, lawyer and lovable wealthy eccentric, Knill was at one time Private Secretary to the Earl of Buckingham and a trustee of his estate. Rumour has it that he was a privateer —

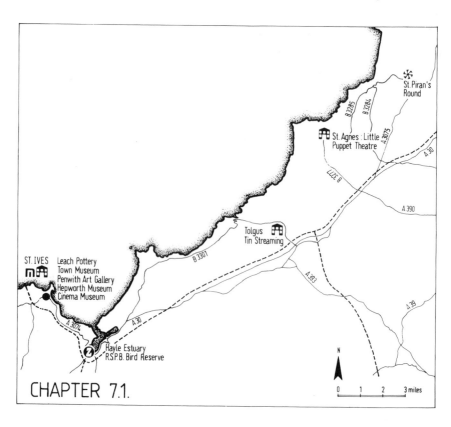

CHAPTER 7.1.

St Ives

having plenty of opportunity, but his memorial lies elsewhere. On his instructions John Smeaton built the sheltering pier and Knill built the Steeple outside the town, fully intending it to be his final resting-place, though he was, as it happens, buried in London.

Everything in the museum is well displayed and the building, too, has an interesting history. The site was originally Wheal Dream copper mine and, like many others, it was unsuccessful; so it was then used to cure and pack pilchards for export to Italy in the mid-nineteenth century. Afterwards the building was extended to become a Bible Christian Chapel, then a laundry and later a cinema. The first floor, however, was retained for maritime purposes when a British Sailors Society Mission used it to house shipwrecked mariners waiting for repatriation.

The Barnes Cinematograph Museum in Fore Street is something quite different. Those interested in this kind of entertainment will find here a complete history of the cinema from the days of magic lanterns.

Five splendid sandy beaches which can accommodate so many people, form a golden crescent setting for the town. On one of them — perhaps all — Virginia Woolf played when she stayed at Talland House, later bringing memories of Godrevy into her book —*To The Lighthouse.* Today St Ives, with its cliff walks, wind-surfing, fishing and sailing, still welcomes visitors to the essential Cornish atmosphere people so enjoy.

The train returns from a small station above Porthminster Beach; as it moves away, Tregenna Castle Hotel — Cornwall's finest — with its castellated turrets, may be glimpsed high above on the cliff top. The next stop is Carbis Bay, which has such fine, smooth sands that it is perhaps the most popular of all. A strange contrast to its appearance of the last century when it was used as a dump for mining waste.

Lelant is an unexpected place, with a

79

quiet individuality that has to be searched for. This perhaps stems from the knowledge that it was a thriving seaport in the Middle Ages, long before St Ives became popular. The church lies behind the Saltings in a village of old-world charm. It is dedicated to St Uny and was the parish church of St Ives until as late as 1826. Inside are interesting memorials to members of the Praed family from Trevethoe, the mansion at the foot of Trencrom. William Praed (1620) and his family are remembered in a slate carving, with kneeling figures, flowers, sand-glass and skull. His famous descendants are Mackworth (whose portrait is in the St Ives museum) and William. The former was the eminent engineer who planned England's canal system, the latter the banker after whom London's Praed Street is named.

Another building of the past is The Abbey in Lower Lelant — a long, low, sixteenth-century construction, and L-shaped, as befits the period.

Quay House — reminiscent of former days — stands beside the Saltings where the A3074 joins the A30. It is an ideal place for birdlovers to study the numerous species there; the RSPB have built an open hide in the grounds. It is available for anyone to use at any time, without obtaining permission from a warden.

The St Ives branch line ends at St Erth, another example of a once proud and busy place. The Star Inn was there in the seventeenth century when the Trewinnards startled everyone by introducing the first private coach to Cornwall. (The vehicle is now in Truro Museum.)

Most drivers hurry through Hayle, glad when they are beyond it, but the present dullness hides one of Cornwall's oldest ports. This estuary has been

---

Places of Interest in and around St Ives

Penwith Art Gallery
Work of the St Ives Society of Artists, originated by Sir Alfred Munnings.

Leach Pottery
Established by Bernard Leach in 1920. Still used as a pottery. His work is also on display.

Barbara Hepworth Museum and Sculpture Garden
Barnoon Hill
Administered by the Tate Gallery, all in the Sculptor's former home.

Town Museum
Wheal Dream
A comprehensive, local maritime exhibition with excellent displays.

Barnes Cinematograph Museum
Fore Street
An unusual collection of exhibits about the history of the cinema from its earliest days.

Lelant Bird Reserve
Quay House
Overlooking the Hayle estuary an open hide is available in the grounds of Quay House.

---

important since Bronze Age times when copper and gold were sent from Ireland to Brittany via St Michael's Mount. Centuries later, when the Industrial Revolution demanded the best in engineering, this part of the world provided it. The old wharves, still visible near the railway bridge, were once part of the great foundry and engineering business belonging to Harvey's — known throughout the world as 'Harvey's of Hayle'. Beside the B3302, which leads out of the square and up Foundry Hill, are remains of this once extensive complex; the hammer mill and old mill pool are easily found.

Today, however, that secondary road derives its fame from the nearby Bird Paradise, which houses a collection of the world's rarest and most beautiful birds, including flamingoes, toucans and colourful parrots flying free.

At Copperhouse the name of a roadside inn is all that is left of former greatness. The romantically-named church of Phillack (St Felicitas) overlooks Hayle Canal. Riviere House on the north side of the Pool was not always a Youth Hostel; Compton Mackenzie and his sister, the actress Fay Compton, spent many childhood holidays there — and loved it.

The huge stretch of towans or sand dunes, which forms part of St Ives Bay is ideal for holiday makers to walk, swim, or laze, although all lifeguards' warnings must be observed. Connor Downs is a sprawling development beside the A30 above Gwithian and many historians think it possible that the ancient city of Connor (Irish for haven) lies there beneath the dunes.

Gwithian itself is a small village with a low-towered fifteenth-century church. The unusual sight of thatch here makes the whole an artist's delight: animal-lovers, however, take pleasure in watching the seals which are seen sometimes at Navax Point, (belonging to the National Trust), beyond Godrevy Lighthouse. The cliffs all round here are turfy and good for walking, but bathers will find that the water is often stained by the Red River, which collects tin waste on its way to the sea.

In 1649, Godrevy Island was the scene of a notable shipwreck. After the execution of King Charles I, many loyal subjects tried to save some of his lace-trimmed garments and other possessions and sent them abroad for safe keeping. Unfortunately, the ship carrying them was wrecked, and only a few of the royal clothes were washed ashore — together with a man, a boy and a dog — the only survivors of the tragedy.

In July and early August, the cliffs of Reskajeage Downs between the B3301 and the sea are brilliant with gorse and heather. Once past the fearful Hell's Mouth, however, walkers along the coastal footpath will find the way easier and safer. The views along the coast towards St Agnes Head and the Beacon are really spectacular on a bright day; sometimes the colours appear too brilliant to be real.

Most of the land between Carvannel Downs and the A30 was once the vast Tehidy estate and belonged to the Basset family till about 1921; their mansion is now a hospital. The monument on Carn Brea, which can be seen for miles around, was erected to the memory of Francis Basset de Dunstanville, a great local benefactor. His main concern was to improve the lot of the numerous poor, especially those who risked their lives gathering the succulent herb that grew in dangerous places on Samphire Island. He built Portreath Harbour in 1760 to facilitate the loading and unloading of copper ore. Before that, the ships had to be loaded from the beach — a very irksome task. But this was, and still is, a coast of storms; so the ancient landmark known as the Pepperpot was a much-needed guide for ships to berth safely. By 1840, when mining was at its peak, the population of this area was about 30,000, busy with all the ancillary industries connected with the extraction of tin and copper. Inland, pleasant minor roads wander up and down towards Portreath and St Agnes.

The section of the North Coast Path

Godrevy

between Portreath and St Agnes Beacon, however, has been described as the finest walk in Cornwall. A short way along the B3300 in the Portreath valley is Tolgus Tin, a unique historic tin-streaming complex still producing its mineral and welcoming visitors to see how it is won: an audio-visual exhibition helps to make the process easier to understand.

Not far away is a very different collection of items about another aspect of local life. It concerns agriculture and shows farm tools and implements which have been used in the area.

Porth Towan and Chapel Porth have fine, sandy beaches, but the undertow of currents is treacherous and lifeguards' warnings must be heeded. All round the National Trust's Chapel Porth and inland for some distance, there are derelict mine buildings in profusion. The heathery slopes of the cliffs still only partly cover the great heaps of waste that have been there for so long. In the mid and late nineteenth century, St Agnes parish was one of Cornwall's most active mining areas, and those who worked there were proud of the boast that *Sten Sen Agnes an gwella sten yu Kernow* — 'St Agnes' tin is the best tin in Cornwall'. All these little 'porths', or landing places, have been used since very early times, and foundations of the chapel traditionally dedicated to St Agnes can still be seen in the cliffs at Chapel Porth.

After several abortive attempts, a harbour was eventually built here in 1793, and the manner of loading the ships was quite ingenious. Stagings were constructed on the cliff face, and cargoes moved by means of a horse-whim. Now all of this has gone, and it is virtually impossible to find any trace of the once busy port: but some evidence of a mining community still remains. The miners' cottages at Stippy Stappy on the steep hill below the church and Wheal Coates engine house on the Beacon (629ft) are probably painted and photographed more often than any other mining building. The handsome Miners' and Mechanics' Institute in the centre of the village is a different reminder of those prosperous years. Built in 1893, one of the first generous gifts of the philanthropist Passmore Edwards, anxious to help the men educate themselves, it is now a club; but inside there are some interesting old mining records.

Next to the Institute is Cornwall's first permanent professional puppet theatre. As well as providing family entertainment, there is a display of local arts and crafts in the exhibition gallery.

In Beaconsfield Place, near the car park, some National Trust property is used in a new way, but perhaps in line with life as it was when the cottages were built about five hundred years ago. A pottery is established here, and the exhibits include items fired with various glazes such as ash, dolomite, tenmoku and celadon.

The St Agnes Model Village, opened in 1973, shows Cornwall in miniature so successfully that someone has commented that it was like standing in the middle of Cornwall and seeing all the beauty spots at once. Models include mining scenes, a small cathedral, Penzance Heliport, the Come-to-Good Meeting House, the new County Hall and numerous others in a suitably landscaped setting complete with the Tamar Bridge carrying its load of cars.

The north coast route continues along the B3285 towards Perranporth but it is worthwhile making a detour down the first lane on the right after Barkla Shop. It is narrow and steep, and motorists should travel slowly, so that they do not miss the picturesque thatched Harmony Cot, birthplace of the famous painter John Opie. Beyond the ford over the Silver River — so named because of its trout — the lane climbs towards the B3284. On the left, before the railway bridge, is Ferndale, a bird rescue station where visitors can see the work being done. In the Agnes Clarke Bird Care section anything from a starling with a broken wing to a puffin that has been blown off course is looked after.

On the coastal side of the B3285 are the headquarters of the Cornwall Gliding Club; just beyond, Cligga Head is exceptionally good for birdwatching. Views from these cliffs rival the Mediterranean in the varied colours of the sea, sand and rock formations. The beauty of Perranporth's beaches is deceptive and many lives have been lost here by those foolish enough to disregard the red flag warnings. Currents, quicksands and the massive power of incoming waves are the dangers, but surfers who take the right precautions can enjoy the three-mile stretch of Atlantic rollers. Away from the dangers, children are catered for with bathing pools, a model-yacht boat pond and various other amusements.

Beyond Gear Holiday Camp, on the north side, there is a handsome area of sand dunes, once visited by pilgrims from many lands. They came to pay homage to St Piran, patron saint of tinners, but eventually his chapel — as old as Iona — was covered by sand. It was rescued in 1835 and protected by a concrete shell, but the elements won again and have finally been victorious. The sands at the extreme end of Perran Beach are now used for military training purposes; visitors can reach Newquay only by inland routes.

The B3285 climbs up out of Perranporth, passing St Piran's Round, an impressive Iron Age fortification, adapted in the Middle Ages for use as a playing place. Revivals of the Cornish miracle plays took place there as recently as 1969-73, when the productions attracted large audiences.

About five miles along the A3075 is Newquay — a lively town with something for everyone in all weathers, voted first among Cornwall's holiday resorts for its magnificent beaches. At low tide these become one bay, but each has a different character when the seas roll in.

Newquay existed as a port in the mid-fifteenth century; the export of pilchards to the Mediterranean was profitable during the seventeenth and eighteenth centuries when the huer's hut below the Atlantic Hotel came into its own. Here, as at St Ives, the cry of 'Hevva! Hevva!' sent fishermen out for the catch, and

their wives home, to bake something quick and warm for their men's return. This was always the traditional slab of plain pastry and mixed fruit now called 'heavy' cake — but its name is derived from the cry, not from bad cooking.

In 1838, Joseph Treffry of Fowey decided to use the shelter of this harbour for his china clay exports and built a new quay. For forty years cargoes came and went, until Par was developed and usurped Newquay's usefulness.

The list of attractions here covers everything holidaymakers expect at a popular resort. Some surprise visitors — particularly the pleasantly situated zoo and leisure park, set in eight acres of landscaped gardens, five minutes away from the town centre. One or two days could well be spent here.

The surfing facilities and cliff walks are perhaps Newquay's specialities, each rocky promontory — as with the bays — having its interest. Towan Head, which stretches out to sea past the huer's hut and the golf course, boasts a small castellated tower and private chapel belonging to the Molesworth family. From here, Cornwall offers another fine two-way expanse of distant coastline. Pentire Point East at the opposite arm of Fistral Bay has good views, too, — a vantage point appreciated by pre-historic man: tumuli remains have been found here.

There are numerous places of interest near Newquay, one being Porth Reservoir off the A3059 to St Columb Major. Along the coast road there are round barrows on Trevelgue Head which lies beyond the bay of Porth on the B3276.

Further north Mawgan Porth's smallness is delightful. The discovery of an extensive Dark Age settlement on the nearby cliffs was of great interest to historians. It was not fortified, and excavations showed courtyard houses, grouped as a Cornish 'trev', or hamlet, where the land sloped to the stream flowing into the bay. Drifting sands apparently forced the inhabitants inland to St Mawgan, but they preserved an unusual quantity of remains for archaeologists. Domestic details were comparatively easy to establish. Pottery finds were significant because, being of North European type, they indicated Cornwall's break with Mediterranean cultures, the result of Arab domination over old sea routes. The remains of the small church or anchorite's cell indicate that this particular settlement had been an important place.

The tranquil Lanherne valley is little-known, though very lovely. Halfway up the valley and in the shelter of long-established trees, St Mawgan village hides its charms. The church has Cornwall's best collection of brasses — mainly of the Arundells, whose former home was Lanherne, the nearby manor house. It has been a Carmelite monastery since 1794; the small chapel is open to the public.

Trevaunance Coombe, St Agnes

The creeper-clad inn opposite seems to have an out-of-place name, The Falcon. Nevertheless it is particularly apt as, during the persecution of Roman Catholics in Reformation days priests celebrated Mass in secret, and the signal to the faithful that it was about to begin would be the freeing of a falcon.

The stream runs quietly through this historic village and beside the bridge is a small shop offering a wide range of gifts. All are of high quality and from Cornish craftsmen.

The road climbs through leafy lanes to another village which has been important in the past — St Columb Major, even considered a possible site for Cornwall's cathedral. The village is perhaps best known now for the Shrove Tuesday Hurling contest when a ball of silver-coated applewood is used in the Town versus Country game. This custom was once a feature of most village feast days, and is believed to have originated as a pagan festival in honour of spring. The handsome church dominates the houses around and, proud of its fourteenth-century foundation, plays host to a popular annual music festival. The Ring O' Bells across the road is a secular reminder of the fine tradition of bell-ringing associated with the church.

After the roundabout at the beginning of the by-pass there is a sign to Castle-an-Dinas, about two miles along the road. Although it has only pedestrian access across private land, it is worth the climb for the panoramic view beyond Goss Moor to the china clay country. These remains of a massive Iron Age fort are some 700ft above sea level and composed of three concentric rings, hedges and ditches. The fact that there is only one entrance emphasises the wisdom of pre-historic builders.

Black and White Cross which lie

Places of Interest in and around Newquay

Porth Reservoir
Off the A3059 Newquay-Wadebridge road; permission for use from SWWA.

Trevelgue Head
A promontory fort with a seven-line defence of banks and ditches.

Lanherne Chapel
St Mawgan-in-Pydar
The entire property once belonged to the Arundells. Since 1794 it has been a Carmelite monastery. Open to the public.

Castle-an-Dinas
2m east-south-east of St Columb Major
An approximately circular fort high above the clay tips and Goss Moor.

Trerice (National Trust)
SE of Newquay
A very attractive small manor house rebuilt in 1571. It has contemporary fireplaces and plaster ceilings.

---

between Castle-an-Dinas and Quintrell Downs may have been named as important stations for pilgrims to Holywell: or perhaps they were depots for the black and white tin streamed from the moorland. In either case Summercourt September Fair would have been involved.

On the A3058 Summercourt to Newquay road, Dairyland offers an unusual look at country life. It is a working farm with 'space-age milking on a merry-go-round' where 160 cows are milked to music in one of Europe's most up-to-date modern rotary parlours. The museum of rural exhibits in another part of the farm displays tools

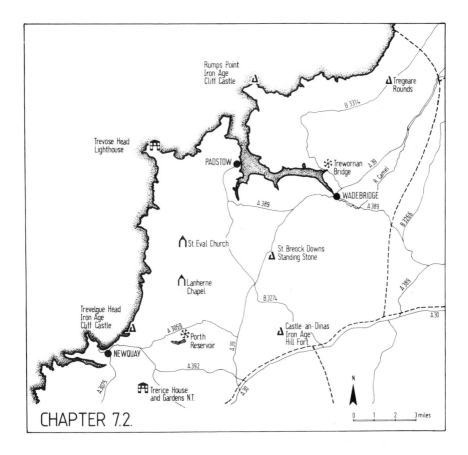

Rumps Point
Iron Age
Cliff Castle

Tregeare
Rounds

B 3314

R. Camel

Trevose Head
Lighthouse

PADSTOW

Trewornan
Bridge

A 39

WADEBRIDGE

A 389

A 389

A 389

B 3266

St. Eval Church

St. Breock Downs
Standing Stone

Lanherne
Chapel

B 3274

A 30

Trevelgue Head
Iron Age
Cliff Castle

A 3059

Porth
Reservoir

Castle · an · Dinas
Iron Age
Hill Fort

A 39

NEWQUAY

A 392

A 30

A 3075

Trerice House
and Gardens N.T.

N

CHAPTER 7.2.

0   1   2   3 miles

and instruments used on farms in the past.

At Kestle Mill a narrow lane winds steeply up to the charming National Trust property of Trerice Manor. Protecting trees stand round this popular house, small enough to be a home, yet retaining the quality and character of the Royalist Arundells who rebuilt it in 1572.

The Lappa Valley Railway takes visitors in a miniature train along part of the original GWR Newquay to Chacewater track. At the end of the short ride to a leisure park, there is the historic engine house and stack of the disused East Wheal Rose mine. This was Cornwall's richest lead-producing works until a cloudburst brought disaster to the miners and closure to the mine.

The road from Newlyn East to Cubert and Holywell is so straight that it probably follows an ancient pilgrim way. The well which gives the place its name is, in fact, not on the beach but about a quarter of a mile away, at Trevornick Farm. This lies behind the extensive dunes set in a wide area of National Trust and Ministry of Defence land — footpaths being clearly defined. The Trust path leads to Kelsey Head and West Pentire on the Newquay side of Porth Joke and is strangely remote, though so near to the busy holiday

Trerice

resort.

Here the cliff flowers are specially delightful in spring and early summer, while the little cove is ideal for families who want to avoid crowds. Its unusual name comes from the fact that it was once the haunt of choughs — *chogha* being the Cornish plural of 'jackdaw', to which family the chough belongs.

Crantock is an attractive village centred on the Round Garden, the little orchard in the middle belonging to the National Trust. Its ancient collegiate church is on a hill overlooking the Gannel.

It is pleasant to walk from here to Cubert Common, one of the few enclosed commons in the country, now National Trust land. Another path follows the line of the Gannel to Trevemper and Newquay, and, though the beach is good for children, it can be dangerous, as the river runs swiftly in under the cliffs of East Pentire. A short and different way back to Newquay at this point is by passenger ferry from West Pentire.

Padstow, the next holiday centre along this north coast, rests quietly on past memories. Buildings here from the Middle Ages are still relatively unspoilt; slate-hung and stone cottages and their colourful sheltered gardens edge the one-way route to the harbour. There, small coasters from the Continent berth beside gaily-rigged yachts, some built locally at Brabyn's Yard. Such a peaceful sight is far-removed from the busy scenes of centuries ago when Padstow was one of the largest towns in Cornwall, on the vital trade route between Ireland and Europe. On the south quay there is still the sixteenth-century courthouse where Sir Walter Raleigh presided as Lord Warden of the Stanneries.

St Petroc, Cornwall's chief saint, settled here in the sixth century, and the church dedicated to him is still mostly unrestored from the fifteenth-century building; its unusual font is made of blue-black Catacleuse stone from the quarries at Harlyn Bay. In nearby Fentonluna Lane are the Tropical Bird and Butterfly Gardens. A recent attraction is a separate walk through an enclosure for both tropical and native species of butterfly; the owners hope to breed them.

Behind the church, screened from the road by a castellated wall is Prideaux Place, one of the few Cornish manor houses still occupied by the family for whose ancestor it was built. That was Nicholas Prideaux who lived in Tudor times. It is not open to the public, but on 1 May, when all the world seems to come to Padstow, the doors are opened to the blue horse of the festival and he dances in the staircase hall to the old traditional tune.

Parking is not easy in Padstow during the season; on May Day it is impossible, especially with crowds lining the narrow streets waiting for the procession of this unique folk festival — Padstow's 'Obby 'Oss. It takes the form of a dance struggle between 'Oss and Teazer and is thought to represent the conflict between winter and summer. Some consider it to be another expression of the fight between good and evil, as seen in the story of St George and the dragon. A short distance from the town a spring dedicated to him is believed to have gushed forth from the rock immediately he set foot there. The reference to the same saint adds credence to the connection. But whatever lies behind the old custom, the procession of horse, teazer, dancers, singers and musicians still makes its way annually between houses decked with flags and greenery.

North of Padstow, above Brabyn's Yard, the public footpath leads to St George's Well, and on to Stepper Point, where the spectacular cliff scenery remains unspoilt. There are tracks all round past Trevone Bay to Trevose Head. Motorists have to shuttle to and from these coastal points, as there is no connecting road. The fine farmstead at the entrance to the hamlet of Treator on the B3276 is memorable as the birthplace of Sir Goldsworthy Gurney, another great Cornish engineer.

After Trevone Bay, with its clean sand, where rock eddies can be dangerous, is Harlyn. It is interesting historically because of the gold lunulae and the many prehistoric remains discovered there early in the twentieth century, when workmen, digging foundations for a house, uncovered a Neolithic cemetery. Some of the antiquities are to be seen in the museum at Truro.

The toll charged to drive to the point at Trevose Head is little enough to pay for some of Cornwall's wildest and roughest coastal views. The lighthouse, the last to be run on compressed air and paraffin, is open daily except Sunday.

Few golf courses can be as well sited as the links at Trevose. Open to the headland, with more than ten beaches and the ruins of the chapel where St Petroc converted Prince Constantine close by, they must be unique.

The coastal footpath is difficult to negotiate along these very exposed cliffs, and agile walkers who venture down the steep path to Fox Cove will find a delightful place of retreat even at the busiest times. The National Trust has saved the cliffs at Porthcothan, and, in 1966, also acquired 220 more acres — the gift of Mr E. Thornton-Smith. That land stretches from Porth Mear, past several fine small coves, a fine rock arch, and, beyond Park Head, to Diggory's Island at the north end of Bedruthan

Steps. These rock stairs became eroded
to danger point but have recently been
restored by the Trust. There is also an
information centre, shop, tea-room and
car park near by.

Arable fields are under cultivation
right to the cliff edge — flocks of sheep
are surprisingly numerous. Tamarisk
hedges, unusual in Cornwall, are planted
here, not for their beauty, but because
they afford the most effective protection
from salt spray blown off the sea during
gales.

After the pleasures of Padstow and its
nearby coast, visitors will find it strange
to be directed to a disused aerodrome.
Nevertheless, it would be a pity to miss
the church of St Eval (pronounced as in
ever), lonely, and surrounded by dreary
concrete flats. On the way there is a sign
to St Eval Leather Crafts — a cottage
industry housed in a neat homestead
where a variety of high quality goods are
made.

The rather severe exterior of St Eval
belies its character. It is, in fact, one of
the most welcoming in Cornwall, with

doors open for visitors. During World
War II, squadrons of Coastal Command
flew from this station, their badge being
a likeness of the church. In March 1959,
205 Squadron presented their standard
to this place of worship, where it still
hangs. The handsome font cover is an
additional reminder of that association.
Today padre and vicar share services as
the congregation is drawn from RAF St
Mawgan and the eighty civilian homes in
this scattered parish.

In complete contrast, St Ervan is
hidden in the wooded seclusion of its
churchtown at the end of a narrow lane
between sections of the old aerodrome.
It is built on a circular Celtic site, high
above a lush valley, with a golden angel
at the door — perhaps it is the saint
himself — inviting you to enter. Inside,
there is the Lord's Prayer in Cornish,
and some fine old slate headstones on
the walls.

From here the lanes wind through
Rumford and over the B3274 to the
parish of St Issey. The rich brown and
red-brown stone quarried nearby is used
locally, its warm colours reflected from
the walls of cottages whose bright
gardens border on the road. Where the
lane joins the A389 Padstow Road, there
is another Ring O' Bells.

Little Petherick takes up a
considerable amount of the A389 from
here to Padstow, but it is such a
delightful village that no one complains.
Old slate-hung houses lean towards the
mill stream, as if sharing a secret.
Possibly they are talking about the small
church. There is little left of the tiny
building that was here six hundred years
before — only two bells, some bench
ends, a font and the thirteenth-century
marble slab to Sir Roger Lemporu,
unusually decorated with a human head
and a foliated cross. Athelstan Riley
became patron here in 1898 and restored

90

building, furniture and vestments to its former High Church tradition.

The jewels, clothes and furnishings lavishly displayed at Penjoly Crafts, just past Little Petherick, are both colourful and of fine quality workmanship, mainly Cornish. Lack of space prevents some of the items being seen to the best advantage but there is so much that at least an hour is needed.

Wadebridge is interesting for several reasons — its name, its position, its bridge and its own pleasant character. Historians believe that *wade* indicated that it had probably been used by the Romans who crossed the River Camel at

that point because of the *vadum* or ford there. In the Middle Ages, before the bridge was built, there was so much traffic at this fording point that chapels were erected to greet the travellers — pilgrims among them — and doubtless also to receive alms. St Michael's at the St Breock end, was licensed as early as 1382, about 1468 a bridge was built between it and the King's Chapel at the eastern end. They were both sold for secular purposes by Queen Elizabeth I in 1591. So many tales exist about the construction of what Carew called 'the longest, strongest and fairest bridge that the Shire can muster' that more needs to

Inn sign, Wadebridge

Wadebridge

be said about it. In 1538, Leland gave the following interesting account:

> Wadebridge wher ther was a fery 80 yeres syns and menne sumtyme passing over by horse stoode often in great jeopardie, then one Lovebone, Vicar of Wadebridge, movid with pitie began the bridge and with great paine and studie, good people putting their help thereto finished it with xvij fair and great uniforme arches of stone. One told me that the foundation of certein of th' arches was first sette on so quick sandy ground that Lovebone almost despaired to performe the bridge ontyl such tyme as he layed pakkes of wolle for fundation.

The Bridge on Wool inn sign agrees with this report; so do those who appreciate that wool solidifies when wet and compressed. Others, however,

believe that money to build the bridge came from wealthy sheep farmers in and around the area, especially those from Bodmin Moor.

The slate quays and stone wharves which can still be seen in some places beside the river are, however, little more than ghostly reminders of the great trading days of the town, situated as it is where the old pilgrims' way to the Mount crosses the trade route from Ireland to Europe. Eventually, railways brought a different kind of traffic — holidaymakers and goods to Wadebridge and Padstow, but the line beside the Camel estuary is now only for pedestrians. It provides a quiet two hours of walking — the new raised swan nesting mounds being of special interest. Buses run from Padstow for those preferring to return by road.

Inland, on the A389 Bodmin road, another old railway line at Sladesbridge

Hingham Mill

offers more quiet walking. This, however, extends very much further over the St Kew Highway and on towards Delabole, Camelford and North Cornwall.

To the south of Wadebridge, the county showground lies on high ground beside the A39 from St Columb. The Royal Cornwall Show is held here in June when Cornish talents compete in every field. Vintage car rallies and all the many other events taking place here are well advertised. The St Breock standing stone is also on these downs.

Wadebridge's parish church of St Breock lies in a tree-encircled valley a little out of the town. It rests peacefully at the foot of the lane which climbs to a cluster of cottages and a pleasant art gallery, which also contains the finest range of high-quality reproduction furniture in Cornwall. To explore the area north of Wadebridge begin at Egloshayle (estuary church) on the A389 Bodmin road. The church itself lies on the corner of a lane. It is an impressive building with an 80ft high tower, a door commemorating the gift of the tower by John Loveybond and a grand east window of five lights.

The lane climbs and twists away to Above Town, where potters can be seen in the Egloshayle Pottery. Turns, first left, then right at the next junction, bring unexpected country and one of the few working corn mills left. The bridge over the River Allen is scarcely the width of a car, a warning of the extreme narrowness of the way ahead to St Mabyn. This is a village of many footpaths, all worthy of exploration. Three miles beyond lies the well-kept St Tudy where there is much to interest visitors. On the side of the church wall is a tablet to Charles, son of John Bligh (who died in 1770) — the grandfather of Admiral William Bligh of 'Bounty and

St Tudy

Breadfruit' fame. Nearby Tinten farm was his birthplace, in about 1753. A recent memorial inside the church is a wooden figure of Our Lord carved from elm grown on the nearby Hengar estate. The artist was Fritz Loeng who came from Oberammergau as a refugee and had taken the part of Christ in its famous Passion Play.

Across the road from the church there is Burleigh's Craft Shop, specialising in paperweights. Immediately behind, craftsmen in the Copper Workshop create beautiful things from one of Cornwall's natural minerals. Their work is displayed in the Craft Gallery.

Not far away is Michaelstow and Bearoak Gardens where a self-sufficiency farm has been created. It looks delightful in the summer sunshine, but as the owners tell you, being self-sufficient is very hard work.

Across the A39 the village of St Teath gathers round its church, built on a circular Celtic site and once an important collegiate institution.

The countryside picture changes now, and open land is much more in evidence as the byways join the B3314 and climb to Tregeare Rounds where the lane before Pendoggett village turns sharply towards the sea. As the road nears the coast, the number of footpaths increases — leading down the valleys and cliffs towards Port Gaverne, Port Isaac and Port Quin.

Each of these has a different history, each important in its way since before Tudor times. Port Gaverne supported a thriving pilchard industry which brought prosperity to Cornish fishermen even as late as the nineteenth century. The National Trust now owns the beach and two groups of cellars, where fishermen used to make and store their pots, nets, sails and gear as well as process their catch.

The name of Port Isaac puzzles visitors and those unfamiliar with the Cornish language. It means nothing more than the corn port (Porthysow) although it once had the second largest pilchard fishery on the north coast and a good trade in slate. Now, its narrow, twisting streets tumble down to the postage-stamp beach where visitors pay to park their cars in season. It is popular with artists, lovers of 'doll's houses' and those who like walking. In its very heart is 'The Birdcage', a delightful high, narrow house — one of the National Trust's recent acquisitions.

From here the coastal footpath keeps faithfully to the cliffs: motorists have to turn inland through St Endellion. The church is another of the many collegiate establishments in Cornwall with an interesting history and fine bench ends.

Places of Interest North of the Camel Estuary

Tregeare Rounds
2m north-north-east of St Kew
A site with a curious slope to the ramparts, suggesting a cattle enclosure rather than defence.

The Rumps (National Trust)
Pentire Point
A fine example of an Iron Age cliff castle — one of the best in Cornwall.

Trewornan Bridge B3314
A deceptive bridge, apparently mediaeval, but in fact Georgian.

The ringers' rhyme in the tower was written by Nicholas Roscarrock, a recusant whose manor of Tresungers nearby still retains its former Tudor grandeur. Today, most visitors to St Endellion to enjoy the annual festival of music and drama held in July.

Port Quin is called the village that died; indeed that is what happened. One day all the men went fishing, were caught in a storm and drowned. The little place is now coming to life as the National Trust has adapted the fishermen's cottages for holiday homes and the cove has a cared-for look.

Seven hundred acres of the land from Trevan Point to the Rumps and Polzeath Beach belong to the National Trust. Saved from development in 1935, this might be called a poet's memorial. Lawrence Binyon sat on this headland and found inspiration for his famous poem *For The Fallen*.

May is a good time to visit Pentire Farm and the Rumps area. Cliff flowers are especially lovely then. This is also one of the few places where pillow-lava, a volcanic rock like pumice-stone, reaches the surface. The ancient ruins are those of an Iron Age cliff castle.

Just below lies Polzeath, fine for surfing and very popular. The Doom Bar opposite Daymer Bay, is composed of sand specially good for fertilising, and has its own legend. The story goes that a mermaid had once guarded Padstow, but after being mortally wounded by a young man, cursed the place, withdrew her protection and caused the sand to pile up and hinder shipping. It does so still, but is now a blessing, because of its benefits to agriculture.

Rock has wide and beautiful sands, an estuary beloved by artists and yachtsmen, as it possesses a rare combination of colour and sheltered freedom. It is a place for sportsmen who tire of the sea, because St Enodoc —

with its strange church — has a golf course close by.

The road back to Wadebridge lies through St Minver, another village famous for its bellringers. Like St Endellion this church has a painted ringers' rhyme and, as further inspiration to churchgoers, an unusual broached spire.

Trewarnon Bridge over the River Amble is of particular interest as it is perhaps the only one in Cornwall built after the Reformation that is really worth examining. It appears to be mediaeval, with pointed arches and handsome piers; in fact, it is little more than 150 years old, having been built by squires who made their fortunes from wealth under the ground.

8 Bodmin and the Moor

The town of Bodmin, Cornwall's geographical centre, stands on the Moor beside the River Camel, where the twentieth-century A30 (by-passed in 1976) crosses the ancient trade route from Ireland to Europe. Its name means 'abode of monks' for the town grew up around the priory which had been built by St Petroc's followers, who settled here in the fifth century. In 1086, Bodmin was Cornwall's only town and has since been a coinage centre, a meeting place for the Assize Courts (still held here), and the home of the County Infantry Regiment. But when Truro became the cathedral city, Bodmin's importance rapidly declined, and an air of regret for what might have been seems to linger in the town.

There are, however, still a number of interesting places to visit, both in and around Bodmin. Perhaps first, St Petroc's is an imposing building — Cornwall's largest parish church, where relics of the saint rest in an ivory casket, which a jeweller recently said he could not value because it was beyond all price. In 1177, these relics were stolen by an Augustinian monk but were later recovered by Prior Roger of Bodmin, as a result of some brilliant religious detective work. Each year, at the annual mayoral elections, these treasures are taken out of the church and carried in procession through the town. At the lower end of the churchyard, down Priory Road, is St Guron's Well, set into the wall at the roundabout. It is believed to be named after a little-known Celtic saint who came here even before Petroc.

A few hundred yards up Turf Street is Mount Folly, probably the original Friary garden, Folly being a corruption of an old word with that meaning. The Great Hall is now the Assize Court and in the nearby Guildhall are two relics from the first building. One is a bell, the other a stone corn-measure bowl inscribed 'However ye sell — BF1563 — your measure fyll.' The nearby Turret Clock is a reminder of what happened after the 1549 Prayer Book Rebellion. It is close to the spot where Nicholas Boyer, Mayor of Bodmin, was hanged for the part he played in the revolt.

Sir Arthur Quiller-Couch (1863-1944), the internationally famous author, was born in Bodmin, where his father, Thomas, was a much-loved doctor. Opposite St Guron's Well on the walls of the Cornish Guardian offices a memorial plaque marks 'Q's' birthplace.

The right fork at the top of Turf Street leads to the 160ft Beacon, a pleasant picnic area with fine views. The 144ft obelisk at its summit commemorates General Walter Raleigh Gilbert, who was given a baronetcy by Queen Victoria for distinguished services in India.

At the top of St Nicholas Street are the War Memorial and The Keep where the Duke of Cornwall's Light Infantry Museum is housed. There is no charge for admission, and it is well worth a visit to see such a varied and interesting collection of standards, guns, medals, and regimental memorabilia covering two hundred and fifty years.

From here Halgavor Road leads down to moorland, where a Mock Mayor's Court was held in mediaeval times. The name, translated from the Cornish,

St Michaels Mount

Windsurfing near St Michaels Mount

Engine house at Trewavas Head

The Cheesewring

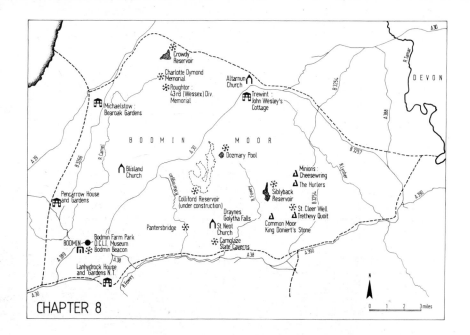

means 'fine for tin streaming and keeping goats', (therefore Goats' Moor). The latest OS map retains the old Cornish name in the area south of Bodmin — Halgavor Moor (SX 072652).

Beyond Halgavor Plantation lies Lanhydrock, which is about two and a half miles south-east of Bodmin. Here is everything visitors could want, for a day of varied pleasure in and around the estate. It is a seventeenth-century house, largely rebuilt after a fire in 1881, superbly sited above the Fowey valley and Respryn bridge. It was one of the most important in Cornwall during the Civil War and held for King Charles when Royalists were encircling the Parliamentarian troops at Lostwithiel in 1644. Four years later, however, although Cromwell's victory was not generally celebrated in Cornwall, Lord Robartes, who had made his fortune from tin, wool and banking, planted an avenue of trees.

The Long Gallery was untouched by the fire; in this 116ft long room the magnificent plaster ceiling depicting scenes from the Old Testament is still in perfect condition. Many acres of garden and woodland were given to the National Trust — the latest as recently as 1970 by the 8th Viscount Clifden. They include Brownqueen Wood which was the monks' deerpark when Lanhydrock belonged to St Petroc's Priory before the Dissolution. The gatehouse (1651) and church are other interesting features of this property.

Two other holiday attractions also lie in this area. One is the Forestry Commission's Silvermine Trail or Bluebell Walk, reached by taking the Fletchers Bridge turning at the first junction beyond Carminow Cross. At that point, in the fields lies Castle Canyke, one of the chain of Celtic Iron Age settlements serving prehistoric tinstreamers and later used on the Ireland to Brittany trade route across mid-Cornwall. The second is Bodmin

Farm Park, well sign-posted after the A38 Liskeard Road. This is a place of family entertainment, where donkey rides, a nature trail, friendly farm animals and a collection of old farm tools give pleasure to most members of the family.

Places of Interest in and around Bodmin

Gilbert Monument
Beacon
A 144ft-high memorial to Sir Walter Raleigh Gilbert.

Duke of Cornwall's Light Infantry Museum
The Keep
It is the county's premier military museum.

Lanhydrock (National Trust)
2½m south-east of Bodmin
A seventeenth-century house, largely rebuilt after a fire in 1881. The gatehouse (1651) and north wing are unaltered. Meals available.

Bodmin Farm Park
Fletcher's Bridge
An ideal place for children; nature trails and friendly farm animals.

Pencarrow
Off the A389 and B3266 at Washaway
Historic Georgian mansion owned and occupied by the Molesworth-St Aubyns. Fine woodlands and a splendid collection of paintings, furniture and china.

The area south-west of Bodmin along the A389 is equally fascinating. Lanivet's Panda inn sign puzzles most people who see it for the first time; but the explanation is simple — the bamboos which thrive in this valley went to the London Zoo to feed a most important animal Chi-Chi. A chapel tower rising mysteriously behind a charming slate-hung house is another of this village's curiosities. It is, in fact, the remains of St Benet's Abbey — a leper hospital in 1411, and a Courtenay mansion in the sixteenth century.

The lane opposite the Panda inn leads to the old Bodmin-Truro coach road — a straight up and over way with fine views at the top. Just beyond the farmstead of Mount Pleasant, as this road joins the A30, a lane on the right leads off into a mass of narrow byways of peace and quiet. Through Lower Woodley and Ruthernbridge, with its ancient packhorse bridge, the lane climbs beside a wildlife sanctuary, past peaceful farms, numerous little unnamed bridges and on to the old granite cottages clustering round Withiel church. In June a Festival of Flowers and Music tempts visitors to linger in this remote village, with its many footpaths branching away from the church.

A short distance on the right along the Roche road is another byway — this one leads to St Wenn, another high and lonely place, but of special interest because of its sundial warning over the porch. Even on a bright day in summer, this place remains solemn. 'Ye Know Not When' say the letters on the face of the old time-keeper. The country all around is green and uncluttered, and the lanes meander across the valley past Rosenannon to St Breock Downs and the prehistoric longstone or, in the brilliance of furze and heather, to Nanstallon, Dunmere and Bodmin.

Along Dunmere Road (A389 to Wadebridge) on the edge of the industrial estate, is The Candle Shop, small but worth a visit. Cornwall's largest selection of candles are all made here, including such unusual items as 'fruit salad' candles which make interesting Christmas gifts.

Farther along the road towards Washaway is the sign to Pencarrow, one of the few fine mansions open to the public and still lived in by the owners. It is in a perfect setting of fifty acres of formal and woodland gardens cared for by the owners, the Molesworth-St Aubyns. The house is reached down a mile-long drive through an Ancient British encampment, under towering beech trees and past fine rhododendrons, camellias and hydrangeas. It is thought to have been built about 1771, but the estate has been in the family since the reign of Elizabeth I.

It is easy enough to reach the centre of Bodmin Moor by driving straight along the A30. Much more interesting, however, is the route through lush lower valleys — in this way its starkness is much more striking. Opposite the ' Hole in the Wall' on the A30 ringroad, Pool Lane leads into Berry Lane and quickly away from the town. The high land gives good views over the River Camel as does Helland, a small village whose church has one of Cornwall's oldest slate memorials. Deep in the valley below is an early fifteenth-century bridge, in fine condition — probably because it is away from a main road and needs no widening.

Not far from the Longstone crossroads on the B3266 is Colesent and the Hollyhill Trust. Here wool from Jacob sheep kept on the moor is spun, woven and dyed. This homely, comfortable farmstead is also run as an educational centre where spinning, dyeing and weaving are taught from the sheep to the garment. Courses in environmental studies are also arranged,

giving priority to those caring for the handicapped, and offering accommodation to groups at YHA prices.

There are two ways to the Moor from here across the Camel which are both delightful. One is Merry Meeting — a place to visit just for the name. Upriver lies Wenford Bridge, so small that many pass it by. From here there is a pleasant walk down the railway track to Dunmere. It is seven miles altogether but even a short stretch is pleasant except on Monday, Wednesday and Friday, when china clay is transported along what is believed to be Cornwall's oldest mineral railway.

Moorland travel consists very much of criss-crossing rivers or avoiding them altogether. From Wenford Bridge it is a question of going a short way south on the east of the Camel, and passing china clay works, crossing the De Lank river to Blisland. Much has been written about this village because it looks different from almost every other in Cornwall. Granite cottages, the Manor House and the old inn round the central grassy area give an expansive look suited to Bilsland's situation on the edge of the moor.

The dedication of the church to St Protus and St Hyacinth is rare; so is the building's beautiful interior, especially its breath-taking rood-screen, restored in 1896 in pre-Reformation style.

Beside the manor house, two roads twist away to the north, and climb higher to the moor, where visitors can find a place to picnic, overlooking the woods of the Camel valley, or wander among the sheep before taking the Bradford road to Kerrow Crafts.

The area round Kerrow Downs is an exciting one. At Bradford an old clapper bridge crosses the De Lank river leading to places with such emotive names as

King Arthur's Downs and Lady Down. Another clapper bridge at Dulphy carries the narrow road over boulder-strewn moorland to St Breward. At 720ft, Cornwall's highest village is close to a region more thickly populated by prehistoric man than anywhere else in the county. Hut circles, stripple stones, stone circles and the unexcavated King Arthur's Hall are all within walking distance. This, like Luxulyan, is another granite village, with stone from nearby De Lank Quarries, also used for London's Blackfriars Bridge, the Wolf Rock, Eddystone and Beachy Head Lighthouses, as well as harbours and other buildings in distant parts of the world.

There are various ways from here to Roughtor, including several moorland paths. The quickest for motorists is to drive down the steep hill into the woods at Tuckingmill and turn either left or right. The latter route which passes eventually through Watergate, is for those prepared to brave some very narrow but lovely lanes. The more straightforward road over the Gam bridge goes right along the B3266 near to Michaelstow and Bearoak Self-Sufficiency Gardens, but at Valley Truckle, just before Helstone, turns to Watergate and the moor again.

Roughtor, sometimes spelt Rowtor, is understandably popular and in the season the small car park is rarely empty. Here Forestry Commission woods are pleasing to the eye in this barren, treeless locality. Near the stream is a monument marking the spot where the unfortunate eighteen-year old Charlotte Dymond was murdered in 1844 by her lover, who was hanged at Bodmin for his crime. The National Trust owns 174 acres of the land about Roughtor which, rising to 1,300ft (400m), is the second highest point in

Cornwall. The remains of its Bronze Age settlement include hut circles and enclosed fields with signs of lynchet cultivation. This tor, given to the Trust in 1951 by Sir Richard Onslow, has the 43rd (Wessex) Division memorial to its men who died in World War II. The bronze tablet is set within foundations of the ruined chapel of St Michael.

Places of Interest on Bodmin Moor between A30 and A39

Blisland Church
Edge of moor
Unusual dedication to St Protus and St Hyacinth. Village green — quite rare in Cornwall. Main feature of church is rood screen.

Bearoak Gardens
Near Michaelstow
A self-sufficiency farm.

Charlotte Dymond Memorial
Below Roughtor
Memorial of young girl murdered by sweetheart, who was hanged at Bodmin.

Wessex Memorial
Roughtor 3m south-east of Camelford
Land given to the National Trust by Sir Richard Onslow in memory of 43rd (Wessex) Division who died in World War II. Bronze tablet at the top.

Crowdy Reservoir
Off A39 Camelford to Bude road
Walks all round, but for other pursuits permits are needed.

The signpost at the crossroads along Jubilee road past Roughtor Farm points to Davidstow. About a mile along is Crowdy Reservoir, which shines a deep

aquamarine on bright summer days. There are opportunities here for windsurfing, and birdwatching from a special hide, but permission must first be obtained from the SWWA.

The sudden flatness of the road through Davidstow Woods is a strange contrast to much of the countryside. Crossing a deserted airfield, it skirts the northern edge of Bodmin Moor along softer lanes leading to Altarnun. Here the old Launceston to Bodmin road used to carry coaches over the picturesque fifteenth-century bridge in the centre of this tiny village, the heart of Cornwall's largest parish. Beside it is the Cathedral of the Moor, a handsome building dedicated to St Non, mother of the Welsh St David. Could it be perhaps that he was born here and not in Wales? The church is as fine inside as out, with seventy-nine Tudor bench ends, and massive piers each made from a single piece of moorstone. Northey Burnard's slate carvings in the churchyard are said to equal the best in Europe. There are home-made teas available here before moving on to Five Lanes, the A30 and Trewint, famed for its associations with John Wesley. A Burnard carving of his

head should be noticed above the Altarnun chapel.

Isbell Cottage, Trewint, lies in a lane which runs parallel to the A30 and it was here that Wesley stayed six times with the hospitable Elizabeth and Digory, conducting services from the stone porch, and on one occasion baptizing one of the Isbell babies. He journeyed to Cornwall in an endeavour to bring people back to the Anglican church, which he begged them never to forsake. But events took quite a different turn, resulting in the establishment of the Methodist movement, which caused the great eighteenth-century schism in the Church of England. After some time the Trewint rooms fell into decay, but in 1948-50, they were restored to their eighteenth-century style. Now a special service is held annually here on Wesley Day, 24 May — others on Sunday afternoons during July and August.

The highest place in Cornwall, Brown Willy, lies behind Jamaica Inn. It is reached only by footpaths, as the nearest road stops as Codda, about a mile from the A30. The source of the River Fowey is between nearby Maiden Tor and Buttern Hill.

Opposite Jamaica Inn there is a road which leads to one of Cornwall's mysteries — Dozmary Pool. In the midst of nowhere, it seems, this area of water is reminiscent of lines by R.L. Stevenson about 'a naked moor, and a shivering pool'. In 1533 Dozmary was reported to be fourteen fathoms deep but no one knows how it exists, as no stream flows into it and it drains no part of the moor. One legend says that there is an underground connection with the sea — its name means Drop of Sea. It has a strange unearthly beauty and an exhilarating brilliance that attracts people whether they want to solve its riddles or not. Two legends remain very firmly associated with this interesting place — one about King Arthur and Excalibur, another of how the villain Tregeagle lost mansion and parklands beneath these waters and was condemned to empty Dozmary using only a limpet shell with a hole in it.

A short distance away at Colliford a new reservoir is under construction, to serve holiday-makers as well as conserving essential supplies of water.

Walkers can cross the moor to Temple, but motorists have to return to the A30 and drive towards Bodmin, turning left on to the old coach road to this hamlet. From the china clay works at Hawk's Tor there is a track which leads through Temple. It was the old way for tinners who, having won their ore from that great granite outcrop, guided laden packhorses down the Warleggan valley to the harbour of Lostwithiel. The simple church stands on the site of a house built by the Knights Templars as a hospice for pilgrims on their way to the Mount. It was that foundation which eventually put it outside episcopal jurisdiction, to become Cornwall's Gretna Green with an unsavoury reputation. That extra-

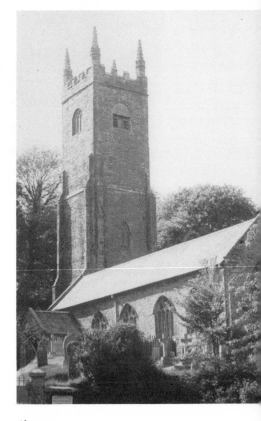

Altarnun

ecclesiastical status continued till about 1744.

To explore the southern area it is advisable to start from Bodmin where the A38 dips into the Glynn Valley woods; there has been a considerable amount of road widening here recently, but it is still delightful, especially in spring and autumn. The road runs close to the Fowey river and provides easy access for fishermen.

At the far end of this valley, from Doublebois, narrow, bouldery lanes, colourful in spring, climb to the quiet grey village of St Cleer which has two interesting features, its handsome church tower, and the roadside holy

102

Trewint

well, carefully restored by Captain Rogers in 1864 as a memorial to his grandfather.

From St Cleer the road leads to Trethevy Quoit standing in a field at the back of some cottages — seeming to guard them. It is a megalithic chamber, 7ft long and about 9ft high. Its shape is that of a capstone supported by five uprights. It is believed to have been constructed some 4,000 years ago by Bronze Age people for use as a burial chamber for their tribesmen. These huge granite slabs were probably taken from the moor but it is not yet known what method was used to place such great weights into position.

Across the road from here is the Trequoit Pottery, with a good display of original stoneware.

Beyond the Crow's Nest hamlet more narrow lanes climb up to open moorland below Caradon Hill. In this landscape of deserted mines, Pensilva seems to be at the top of its own quiet world. Yet in the mid-nineteenth century it and the surrounding villages were so crowded that they looked more like the mining camps of Colorado and the far West. Today the moors are for sheep and for those who enjoy walks away from roads. It is a pleasant, easy path up to Caradon,

Places of Interest on the Central Moorland

Altarnun Church
Off A30 at Five Lanes
Known as the 'Cathedral of the Moor'. Carved memorials in churchyard by Northey Burnard in slate. Unusual jester and fiddler on pew ends in church.

Trewint
Off A30
A place of pilgrimage for Methodists. John Wesley stayed here several times during his evangelising journeys to Cornwall. On 24 May open-air services are held here. This cottage is not a museum but has many treasures.

Dozmary Pool
About 2m from Bolventor, turn off A30
A place of mystery first used by Neolithic man — hundreds of artifacts have been found here. Associations with King Arthur and Tregeagle.

Colliford Reservoir
Near Dozmary Pool
At present under construction — a delightfully sited area.

103

Trethevy Quoit

where, as well as views to Brown Willy, Plymouth and Dartmoor, there are blueberries to pick in summer.

North of Pensilva are Caradon Town and Linkinhorne, once both busy mining centres, but the former is now only a handful of houses. Linkinhorne church, set in its frame of trees, has an unusually handsome granite tower and fine wall paintings, discovered as recently as 1891, and representing the Seven Works of Mercy and the Seven Deadly Sins. Here, too, is Daniel Gumb's memorial. He was a unique Cornishman who lived with his wife and children in a house built under a granite slab near the Cheesewring on the moor. But he was no idler. He taught himself mathematics and the works of Euclid in order to study astronomy, working out the more complicated geometric problems on rocks. His carvings can still be seen by those with really keen eyes.

Beyond Coad's Green on the B3257 a narrow lane on the left leads downhill to Trebartha and East Moor. From the Barton a lane ends in lonely moorland high among prehistoric hut circles. There are paths everywhere and numerous places to explore —

Smallacombe Downs being particularly exciting with its views over King Arthur's Bed and the Fowey river on the far side.

Twelve Men's Moor is here, too — an ancient tin-streaming area known for seven centuries by that name. History records that in 1284 the Prior of Launceston granted a lease there to twelve hard-working tinners. Among them were men with names that deserve to be recorded, such as Boglawoda, Cada, Foth, Trewortha and Broda.

The road from Berriowbridge to Henwood, so busy in the past, is wooded and delightful, climbing up again to moorland. It is so peaceful, yet so full of memories, with old engine houses and mine chimneys.

At Minions parts of an old mineral railway track can still be seen, and in numerous places nearby there are Neolithic and Bronze Age monuments. Paths from this hamlet lead to the Cheesewring where, until the 1950s, quantities of silver-grey granite were quarried and sent to Liskeard and Looe to be exported. But today the place serves a different purpose. It is used by naval apprentices learning the

Places of Interest on Bodmin Moor East of Fowey River

St Cleer Well
In 1858 water flowed from here, but only into a muddy pool to which villagers brought their cattle. Lt Henry Rogers RN bought the land because of the chapel ruins on it, later restoring it.

Trethevy Quoit
Near St Cleer
A handsome prehistoric burial chamber of five standing stones and a capstone. Free access at all times.

Cheesewring
Near Minions
Not a prehistoric monolith, but a natural formation of rock weathered to this shape. The nearby quarry is used by the Royal Navy to train men in absailing.

The Hurlers
Near Minions
Three Neolithic or very early Bronze Age stone circles. The arrangement of these ancient megaliths has given rise to the usual legend of men turned to stone for playing on Sunday. Excavation at the nearby Rillaton Barrow revealed a gold cup, now in the British Museum.

King Doniert Stone
Common Moor
This finely preserved wayside monument to King Doniert has a clearly defined pattern of interlacing on both cross shafts. Probably of the ninth century.

Siblyback Reservoir
1m from Common Moor
An extensive recreational area with space for walks and relaxation even for those without SWWA permits.

disciplines of absailing into the 150ft quarry — a skill which might later save their lives. But the main fascination of this place for most people is the strange stone formation called the Cheesewring, large thick oval slabs which balance precariously. The rocks, about 22ft high and 17ft in diameter have been formed by nature and weathered over the years to their present fantastic shape.

Beside Minions is Caradon — its modern television mast at the top of the 1,210ft (369m) hill. On the right, past the houses, is a notice to The Hurlers Stone Circles, cared for by the Department of the Environment. These strangely-shaped stones have, not unnaturally, given rise to local legends. Were they, in fact, as is supposed, men who played the old game of hurling on a Sunday, and, disobeying the rules of their religion, called down the wrath of the gods upon them? Whatever the legend says, the facts are that these shapes suit their environment and add to the feeling of Cornwall's past that lingers still on Bodmin moor.

At Common Moor a lane on the right leads to Siblyback Reservoir, one of the best recreational reservoirs in Cornwall. Those who want to fish or sail have to obtain permission from the SWWA; but otherwise there are walks and picnic areas for the general public.

There is another Department of the Environment site at the roadside just beyond Common Moor. Here, however, are actual historical records carved on two granite monoliths. One is inscribed with the Latin words DONIERT ROGAVIT PRO ANIMA — 'Doniert prayed for his soul'. He is thought to have been Durngarth, King of Cornwall in the latter half of the ninth century.

Redgate lies at the crossroads, where there is a signpost to Draynes, (originally Drayness) — its bridge was

probably the first over the Fowey. It was recorded in 1362 and carries a very ancient track from Caradon to Bodmin. Here a car park is close to the footpath which leads through dense beech woods to the Golitha Falls. The water cascades for over half a mile of twisting cataracts and the Fowey is seen in majestic splendour. Remember that the pronounciation is Goleetha; it means obstruction.

The Draynes to St Neot road is undulating, sloping steeply to this out of the way village. High beside the road stands the church dedicated to a kindly dwarf. The interior is famous for its well-preserved fifteenth-century and early sixteenth-century stained glass conveying the impressive beauty of pre-Reformation windows. They tell the story of religion from the Creation, but the windows of St Neot and St George were later additions.

Although there is little now to indicate a busy industrial past, St Neot and the Loveny Valley were much involved with the wool trade as well as silver, copper, tin and slate. A short distance down the wooded valley are the Carnglaze Caverns, known to have been worked from ancient times. Visitors taken round on guided tours can see another aspect of the Cornishman's skill when confronted with the need to 'win' any

Places of Interest on Bodmin Moor West of the Fowey River

Golitha Falls
3m north of Dobwalls
Here the Fowey cascades through deep woodland over shelves of smooth rock. There are parking facilities by the road at the entrance to the falls.

St Neot Church
2m north of A38 Glynn Valley
Rare dedication to a pious dwarf. Probably a Cornish hermit who loved animals, as suggested by the windows. Seventeen stained glass lights are priceless — dating from the sixteenth century.

Carnglaze Slate Caverns
Near St Neot
Underground slate caverns of unknown extent, though work has been done here for over two hundred years. A startling lake rivals Capri's Blue Grotto.

Pantersbridge
2m east of St Neot
Interesting double bridge over two streams which carried the old coach road from Liskeard to Bodmin. Possibly originally known as Jesus Bridge.

substance from under the surface. One of the surprises is the great lake, a sight as dramatic as the Blue Grotto on Capri.

The road back to the moor leaves St Neot and climbs to Goonzion Downs and Pantersbridge — a name with a double meaning. The charter of 1241 mentions a place on the high road to Bodmin called Pontiesu named by the Knights Templars as JESUS BRIDGE or PONTJESUS and later corrupted to Pantersbridge. It has charm in its own right, and the second roadway, which eventually took the increasing traffic from Liskeard to Bodmin, adds to its character.

Due north is a farm track to Warleggan — one of the names Winston Graham used in his *Poldark* books. The village is today a desolate, ghostly place, almost deserted, perhaps because the last resident vicar, disapproving of the congregation, locked them out of the church and afterwards preached to cardboard figures.

The way back to Bodmin passes through Mount and Cardinham. Here two ruined castles retain echoes of ancient nobility.

9 North Cornwall

Robert of Mortain established Launceston as Cornwall's northern gateway when, in about 1067, he built his strategic keep over the river. He probably constructed Polston Bridge at the same time, thus re-routing the ancient pilgrim way from Kilkhampton. An early Borough Charter calls the new road *Via Regalis Cornubiensis* — the 'Royal Cornish Way'. The Department of the Environment is responsible for the maintenance of Launceston Castle with its cylindrical keep and ruined walls.

Immediately below, in Castle Street, is Lawrence House Museum, a handsome period building full of exhibits relating to the history of the town and locality. It is one of Cornwall's best museums and the moulded ceilings are both elaborate and beautiful.

A steep road — with one-way traffic, downhill — leads up to the parish church past the Cornish Cobblers. A different kind of shoe-repairer's, where the only leather used comes from the Grampound Tannery — no other is good enough; only bark-tanned skins are adequate.

The church of St Mary Magdalene was built under tragic circumstances. Sir Henry Trecarrel owned an estate a few miles south of the town but lost his wife and son while building his manor. Grief-stricken, he turned to religion, and devoted his wealth to the needs of the church. Particularly noteworthy is the superbly carved granite stonework. The exterior has not an inch without decoration — unusual anywhere, but especially with hard granite. The motifs vary from prayers and angels to roses,

pomegranates and coats of arms — those of Trecarrel and Kelway are on the upper storey of the south porch.

Streets in Launceston are short, and, although Southgate is two roads away, it is, in fact, reached in a minute. This handsome Norman arch — all that remains of the defences — has been widened. Above it and up steep steps are rooms with history. Former guard rooms and prison cells are now an art gallery.

Visitors who see Launceston on

Launceston Museum

market day will be very much aware of the White Hart, where so much happens. It is believed that the entire doorway probably came from the castle chapel — perhaps in 1646, when the stronghold fell to Cromwell's forces.

This pleasant town is a good starting point for the northern area, particularly so for the pack-horse bridge lanes which run south, beginning at the A384 to Tavistock. Immediately there is lush country on this road to Greystone Bridge.

The sharp slate hedges in these parts are screened by ferns — many and varied — and lanes meander peacefully by remote places like Lawley Bridge and Beale's Mill, with its newly-restored well, to Tutwell and Horsebridge. After Greystone, the Tamar winds through deep valleys, but they widen here. The name was once Hautes Brigge, then Hawte Brig.

Since 1377 Stoke Climsland and much of the land in the neighbourhood have belonged to the Duchy of Cornwall — including the church patronage. The first Duke, the Black Prince, was a good landlord, much concerned with the responsibilities of his estates, and in

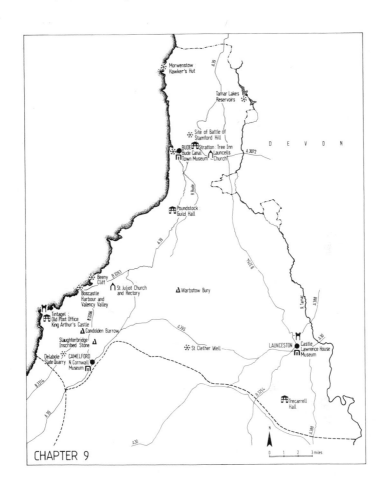

CHAPTER 9

1352 he gave six oaks from this deer park towards the construction of Stoke Church. This is a fine building, standing centrally in the village, above rolling pasturelands and rural countryside: it has a feeling of quiet contentment, as does the village shop opposite: here low beams and cool windows are part of its charm. Little can have changed since this cottage held a position of importance in 1839, when it was appointed the Penny Post receiving house for the district. Before that, it had been a dwelling for workers attending to repairs at the church.

A footpath opposite the church leads to Duchy Home Farm land — a place where many prize-winning cattle are now bred. At the left-hand side of the road towards Kelly Bray a black horse's head on the garage indicates a place called Shutta — it is set back from the road and is easily missed. This sixteenth-century farmhouse is now the base for Cornovi Creations — items made from the Cornish national tartan.

About a mile north of Bray Shop a lane leads off the B3257 to the quiet countryside of Trebullet. Charles I stayed at Trecarrel Hall on his way to do battle at Liskeard. The bridge is not the one that he crossed — that was swept away by flood waters in 1847. Visitors may see Sir Henry's great banqueting hall at Trecarrel. He built it to last — the great beams on its cradle roof are as strong as when they were first lifted there. This might have been another Cotehele but for the two deaths that changed everything. The chapel is also here, with its gallery, for the lord of the manor and his lady when they attended Mass. Perhaps the saddest sight is the pile of great stones lying by the farm gate, where they were left almost five centuries ago.

The B3254 runs back to Launceston

Places of Interest in and around Launceston

Launceston Castle
A fine ruin overlooking the town. It was the chief seat of Robert of Mortain, brother of William I. Impressive views.

Lawrence House Museum
Castle Street
A period building given to the National Trust in 1964 by Mrs G.W. Kittow to preserve the character of the street. The moulded plaster ceilings are exceptional. It is let to the local Borough Council as a museum.

St Mary Magdalene Church
Built in 1511-24 entirely by Sir Henry Trecarrel after the loss of his wife and son. Probably unique in having a granite exterior so elaborately carved. Monuments of interest inside.

Trecarrel Hall
South of Launceston
The banqueting hall is one of the most spectacular domestic buildings of its period in Cornwall.

---

through the broad open fields of South Petherwin. Botathan witnessed scenes of ghosts and exorcism in the seventeenth century.

The hilltop church of Lewannick is built of a stone which is not seen in many places. It is dark green and was quarried at Polyphant across the A30. The churchyard is almost circular — a sure sign of a very early Christian site, possibly as early as the fifth century AD. Here are two 'gravestones' with inscriptions in both Latin and Ogham — an ancient British and Irish alphabet of just twenty letters.

Not many visitors go along the lanes to Laneast, though Sir John Betjeman

called the church an unspoilt version of Altarnun. It was Norman foundation, reconsecrated in the fifteenth century when the thirty-eight pew ends were carved. Today it is very much loved and cared for, with fresh flowers set about to scent the building.

There are walks from here to St Clether, but for the motorist the road runs along a ridge dropping to the church, its holy well, a small hall and one house. There is a serenity in this remote but attractive place. The Lord's

Prayer in Cornish is in the church; its stained glass window of the saint and its sturdy pillars make a visit almost a pilgrimage.

Sheep are very much part of the landscape round Launceston, especially north of the A395 where Treneglos hamlet, reminiscent of a Cornish trev is no more than a tiny green beside a church and two or three houses. It is almost as high as nearby Wilsey Downs, where there are walks and prehistoric tumuli. Celtic tribes were forced to seek safety and live above the wooded valleys — Warbstow Bury, north from Wilsey and Treneglos, is a good example of this and ranks with Castle an Dinas and Chun as one of Cornwall's largest ancient sites: the area is fine for walks on a sunny day.

From this expanse of fields and farms the lane plunges deeply down, between hedgerows not despoiled by harsh council hedgecutters, to Tuckingmill near Canworthy Water on the River Ottery. Fleeces from farms on the high ground once kept these mills busy and the villagers in full employment. Now the cottages are quiet, those beside the river reflecting on their changed position in life.

The road from South Wheatley to

Places of Interest East of Launceston

St Clether Well
¼m north-west of church
Lovely setting above the river in an isolated field. The well building is the largest in Cornwall, with a chapel and stone altar.

Warbstow Bury
3m north of A395 Launceston-Camelford road SX 201909
An impressive pre-historic defensive earthwork: fortress, double-walled and two gateways protecting barrows — King Arthur is said to be buried there.

North Petherwin is narrow and undulating, but wooded and pleasant. After much study, St Paternus came to this place in the sixth century, and the small churchtown remains apart from the main group of houses at Petherwin Gate, in a typically Cornish manner.

Boyton, once a thriving town, has now shrunk to a hamlet. It stands on high ground overlooking the Tamar and part of the old Bude Canal. The parish is proud of Agnes Prest of Northcott, a Protestant martyr, burned at Southernhay in Exeter in 1557 for refusing to accept the doctrine of transubstantiation. She shares a memorial with Thomas Benet outside Maynard School in the city but Boyton is still hoping to have her remembered in her parish church — so far unsuccessfully. The village smith keeps the key and takes great pleasure in showing visitors this small, mediaeval place of worship with its unusual dedication to the Holy Name.

There are numerous walks here, some on high ground and others close to, and even along parts of, the long-defunct Bude Canal.

Motorists returning to Launceston pick up the B3254 road at Ladycross, probably once associated with Tavistock Abbey, and return to Launceston over the Yeolmbridge. This is Cornwall's oldest and most perfectly finished bridge, the only one with a ribbed vault and pointed arches, similar to that of the north gate of Launceston Castle.

On the hill north of the River Kensey and level with the castle, is St Stephen's — once a collegiate establishment and consecrated in 1259, which makes it the mother-church of Launceston. Today, this area of the Kensey valley keeps a little of its past, with a packhorse bridge, slatehung cottages overlooking the mill complex and a toll house; this was where

Launceston's wealth once lay. The building of St Thomas was formerly the chapel of St Stephen, and stands now as the lone reminder of Lanson's pre-Conquest religious past.

The rest of north Cornwall can be divided into two sections, each with a character of its own. Camelford, about sixteen miles north-west of Launceston along the A395, can be a base for seeing the King Arthur country. Motorists driving north from Wadebridge on the A39 approach this quiet market town through the lovely Allen Valley, a route starred with primroses and bluebells in spring.

A peaceful place now, Camelford was once a lively pocket borough, busy with wool and cloth-making as indicated by the nearby Valley Truckle (Cornish for tuckingmill). Sheep have always been plentiful here — not camels, as the town hall's weathervane suggests. That is the practical result of the way mediaeval heralds worked this animal into the town's arms, a play on the name of the river. Well-signposted from the A39, and worth a visit, is the North Cornwall Museum and Gallery. This exhibition opened in 1973, in an old coach house,

---

Nanjizal, near Land's End

St Mawes Castle

The Egyptian House, Penzance

Delabole slate quarry

to display a collection of items reflecting rural life in North Cornwall. A section of the building has been constructed to resemble a typical moorland cottage interior; craft and painting exhibitions are held throughout the season: it was given the Pilgrim Trust Award for the best small museum in England. Next door, too, is something of interest — though entirely different. The shop, Pin Linni Prints, is an out of the way boutique, where original clothes, toys and household goods are printed by hand, using silk screen methods on natural fibres.

The westward coast roads from Camelford all pick up the B3314. On this road is Delabole, between two and three miles away, and well signposted. The village is clean and attractive, but the focal point is the slate quarry which has been producing fine slate for centuries. Pack saddle donkeys were first used to remove the rock, horses were used later and now lorries provide the transport. The great quarry is 500ft deep, and over a mile and a half round. Richard Carew included it in his 1602 Survey of Cornwall, John Wesley wrote about it in the eighteenth century, and Eden Phillpotts made it the subject of his novel *Old Delabole* (1914). The skills they admired are still practised today, and masons produce items such as church altars and fine flooring, memorial stones and plant holders. There are guided tours for visitors, and demonstrations of slate-splitting with 'bettle' and 'chisel'. The name of the local inn has strong links with the quarry, being known as The Bettle and Chisel. After learning about the names of various slate tiles — Ladies, Countesses, Duchesses, Queens, Rags and Imperials — it is interesting to see them used on the old cottages and walls for many miles around.

Northwards along the B3266 the road crosses the high plateau of Waterpit Down, pleasant with extensive views and the ubiquitous sheep. A roadside cross here is a tenth-century stone carved with interlaced ornamentation. It has weathered considerably since it was set up as a pilgrims' waymarker. A maze of narrow lanes leads eventually to Lesnewth, very remote, but once an important place where Cornish kings and chieftains held court (Lis means court or palace, and Noweth/Newth means new). The church is securely built into the hillside opposite a farm and is easily missed, as the roof is at road level.

Only paths lead away from this unusual churchtown, and motorists meet the Boscastle road at the head of the Valency Valley, partly owned by the National Trust. The drop down to St Juliot's church is steep, but typical of roads in this area. The building was in a ruinous condition when Thomas Hardy arrived in 1870 to inspect it and draw up plans for its restoration. This he did, and it was re-opened two years later, as the patron of the living had advanced matters by giving some two-thirds of the building costs. Lovers of Hardy's works will know how the famous man returned again and again to court the rector's sister Emma Gifford and how she persuaded him to leave architecture for literature and later married him in 1874. Beeny Cliff, Buckator, Penally and Pentargon are among the places he loved and incorporated in his first novel.

Places of Interest connected with Thomas Hardy

St Juliot Church
Head of Valency Valley
Dedicated to St Julitta, this isolated building was restored by Thomas Hardy in April 1872. The brass and ruby oil lamps he installed are in Wellington Hotel, Boscastle.

St Juliot Rectory
When Hardy was working there, he stayed with the rector and returned to court his sister-in-law, Emma.

Beeny Cliff
North of Boscastle
Much loved by Hardy and Emma — she sketched it and he wrote from there: 'the opal and the sapphire of that wandering western sea'.

Boscastle Harbour
One of Hardy's poems describes a cliff outline — resembling the neck, head and beak of a bird of prey. Opposite the bathing pool.

Valency Valley
Five miles long — some National Trust. Still lovely and unspoilt.

Many of his poems also contain memories of this period in his life which was not always happy.

At Boscastle, the original inner harbour was built by Sir Richard Grenville in 1584; with sixty-one acres of adjoining cliffs it is National Trust property. It is hard to believe that it was once Launceston's port for shipping slate, corn and tanning bark. Cargoes of food and coal were imported. Today, few would care to negotiate even a small motor yacht between the sharp, twisting rocks of this narrow inlet, but local boatmen who know the dangers take visitors out to see a different view of the cliffs, especially the one some call King Arthur's head.

Steep, heather-and gorse-clad cliffs and a narrow strip of water make Boscastle. Little enough, it is very popular; no doubt the Museum of Witchcraft adds to its appeal. Matters of the past, perhaps, but there are those who say that the black power is still very potent in the area, and agree with the notice on the door of the museum — 'These things happen today'.

The Valency Valley runs inland for five miles.In spring it is a delight — in autumn, unbelievably beautiful. One hundred and thirty-two acres of it are National Trust, including Sentry Ground, the ancient sanctuary ground of Minster Church. Nearby Forrabury Common is a unique survival of Celtic land tenure in long rectangular plots known as 'stitches'.

The cliff walks from here to Tintagel are nothing less than splendid, especially on a fine spring day when there is a profusion of wild flowers and a mass of sea-birds. In June, puffins can be seen on Long Island but not, alas, without binoculars. Rocky Valley, the walk from these cliffs to Trevalga, is one of exceptional beauty. In fact, a whole day could be spent here. Motorists climb out of Boscastle to arrive at Trevalga (the head of Rocky Valley) along the B3263.

Here is a range of man-made pleasures to enjoy in addition to the natural ones. Neighbour to the centuries-old Trethevy Manor is St Nectan's Pottery, where delicately-tinted items are made every day. In the same complex is the St Piran's Gallery and Studio — a permanent exhibition in an unusual fourteenth-century walled garden setting.

Behind the manor a narrow lane climbs high above Bossiney Haven, giving fine views of a great coastal sweep of cliffs. It is the way to St Nectan's Glen, Valency Valley in miniature, and St Nectan's Kieve (great bowl). This is a beautiful valley walk, leading back to the main road.

Bossiney village is now a quiet hamlet but in 1584 it was the centre of a rotten borough whose MP was Sir Francis Drake. A brief detour here leads to Fernleigh Woodcraft where in a slatehung cottage woodturning skills have been practised for many years.

It is difficult to know where Bossiney ends and Tintagel begins because of recent buildings. Many suggest that Tintagel should be avoided, as commercialism spoils the memory of King Arthur. Perhaps there are too many gift shops here, but there is also much to enjoy. In the centre is the Old Post Office, one of the National Trust's most picturesque properties. This small fourteenth-century stone house, with an ancient slate roof of fairy-tale curves, was built on the plan of a mediaeval manor with a large hall. It is called the Post Office because it was the letter receiving office for the district, opened by the GPO in 1844.

A dusty, easy slope (a Land Rover is available for those who prefer it) takes visitors to the foot of Tintagel Head, which is Duchy of Cornwall property. On this magnificent promontory are the well-preserved remains of a Celtic monastery as well as the ruins of one of the Black Prince's castles.

The Department of the Environment has charge of another castle — on the land overlooking the narrow division between cliff and headland. This is the remains of a mediaeval stronghold built by Earl Reginald of Cornwall. On the other side of the valley is King Arthur's Castle Hotel, an outstanding place built to accommodate holidaymakers flocking here as a result of Alfred Tennyson's Arthurian poetry. Even in 1897 this building was thought to detract from the spirit of the area and the fourteen-acre headland was eventually bought for the National Trust as a memorial to the Poet Laureate. Away from the village is the church of St Materiana. It is a fine Norman building, and should be visited when walking along the Glebe cliff.

After leaving Tintagel by the B3263, there is a lane to the left beyond Penpethy Farm which is worth exploring. For archaeologists the lonely mound of Condolden Barrow is an intriguing monument.

Across the B3266 at Slaughterbridge is Worthyvale Manor, an ancient and beautiful place with modern interests of a farm trail and trout farm on an estate crowded with history. It was recorded in the Domesday Book of 1086, but was important even before that for King Arthur is said to have led his Celtic forces into battle against Mordred here. Both were killed and a large stone, inscribed in Latin, still lies on the river bank giving the name Slaughterbridge — an irrevocable link with the past, even though historians consider it to be merely legendary. Later, however, in 823, another decisive battle took place in Worthyvale fields when the Saxon leader Egbert was victorious and later became the first king of all England.

Those who live in Bude in the far north of Cornwall; do not consider their pleasant town to be at all remote or forgotten; it is an area with its own special character and quite different from any other part of the county: a friendly, attractive place, offering a warm-hearted welcome to visitors.

In the 1830s Sir Goldsworthy Gurney built the toy-like castle beside the beach. Today it houses the offices of the Town Council, which maintains the building, keeps the gardens colourful and has transformed the former gardener's shed into a cafe and information area. Adjoining this, the old forge beside the canal has become the town's museum displaying a wide variety of historical and folk exhibits.

The museum is appropriately sited on the lower wharf facing Bude's Canal, which was built in 1826 by Sir Thomas Acland. This canal was almost unique in Britain, as it was not primarily built to carry goods to the coast, but to transport huge quantities of shell sand inland to 'fertilize' or sweeten the acid soil and so improve large areas of land. The original thirty-mile stretch from Bude to Launceston carried barges fitted with wheels and these were hauled up

inclines by stationary steam engines.
Bude, however, did not become a canal
port. It developed into a fine holiday
resort, and visitors now park their cars
beside the canal and watch raft races
that take place on it. They may also fish
there because it is regarded as one of the
finest coarse fishing waters in the west.
A two and a half mile of quiet and level
walking along the tow path is not only
pleasant but also of special interest for
lovers of wild life. About half a mile
along a bird hide has recently been
erected.

Ebbingford Manor, the town's oldest
house, dating from the twelfth century,
is off Vicarage Road, which runs beside
the canal. This one time home of the
Arundells, related to Henry VIII and
Lord Baltimore, founder of Maryland, is
sometimes open to the public.

It is hard to believe that wrecks were a
terrifying commonplace in the early days
of the nineteenth century, for the
pleasures of Bude which include golf and
twelve tennis courts for visitors, are only
for relaxation. There is safe saltwater
swimming in the pool, while beyond the
castle are sands and surf comparable to
those of South Africa and Australia.

Marhamchurch lies south of Bude and
across the A39, through high-banked
hedges and narrow climbing lanes. It is
an unusual rectangular village set on a
ridge, and seems to be keeping watch
over the surrounding farmland. Its wide,
central road leads to the Norman
church, low and square near the War
Memorial. The solid fifteenth-century
oak door is always open and is one of its
interesting features, as is the encased
sanctuary knocker. A former rector,
Brother Peter, came from the Abbey of
the Cross at Bordeaux and was the
incumbent in 1458. His ministry was
apparently so happy that after his death
his ghost returned to the old Rectory,
where he has often been seen — even in
this century.

Village celebrations are the same here
as at all other churches with Celtic
origins — their feast day usually follows
the church festival. The tradition at
Marhamchurch is a rare one. On Revel
Day, after 12 August, Father Neptune
crowns a local schoolgirl who then rides
through the village on a white horse.

Jacobstow church, embraced by trees
in a roadside dell, is easily missed; the
unspoilt hamlet is charming because of
its very solitude. Nearer the coast the
wooded lanes are lost in high open fields
again.

Wainhouse Corner is a junction on
the A39 where the way leads to the
fearful cliffs of Crackington Haven; for
a considerable distance, north and
south, the coastal footpath crosses
National Trust land. This tiny cove was
a harbour for colliers in the eighteenth
and nineteenth centuries; their captains
must have been intrepid sailors to
navigate here. Cambeak on the south
stretches into the sea like a great lizard,
and gated paths lead to Trevigue, a
sheltered farm providing good teas. Cars
may be left here if a further walk to High
Cliff is intended. This is Cornwall's
highest coastal point and the views are

typical of this northern area.

Northwards, on the cliff out of the Haven, stands St Gennys church. It is almost alone in its fold of green fern on the cliffside, and ornamental cherry trees give it a fairytale look in spring. One of the treasures here is the altar tabernacle, a splendid piece of church furniture. Handsomely embroidered kneelers also add to the glory of this Celtic church, where prayers have been said since St Gennys established his humble cell on these cliffs.

The road to Millook, narrow, steep and badly cambered in places, can be negotiated with good brakes and the use of bottom gear. Once safely out of the valley, the wide road past the common falls away to a startling panorama across Widemouth Bay and north to Morwenstow.

Inland from this striking coast lies Poundstock church, guildhall and lych gate. Gentle enough now, it was not so in the fourteenth century when local villains were commissioned as Collectors of Subsidies and lawbreakers wielded more power than good citizens. Affairs reached a climax in 1358, however, when armed men swarmed into the church as a priest was celebrating Mass, killed him at the altar and 'desecrated the vestments and sacred vessels'. It was not long before the killers were caught and punished, and Poundstock returned to peace again; it still retains much of its mediaeval beauty. The guildhall served many purposes: poorhouse, school, substitute church and, today, a meeting place for the parochial church council. The windows are original and worth studying.

The spectacular sands of Widemouth Bay stretch away almost endlessly. Once they were dreaded by sailors, but today visitors can enjoy adventure holidays here and learn canoeing and wind-surfing.

Cornwall has not revealed all its treasures yet — there is much to see between Bude and Morwenstow. Some say that this area is the best of all. The A3072 road goes to Stratton, which, though it has now fallen below Bude in status, was important in Roman times. Its character, however, is quite different. It is rightly proud of Anthony Payne, the Cornish giant who was born at The Tree Inn, and died there, too. This huge man, who weighed 532lb, has a portrait by Kneller in Truro Museum. He devoted his life to the service of his master, Sir Bevil Grenville, whose troops defeated the Roundheads at the Battle of Stamford Hill in 1643. A plaque on the wall marks the site.

Away from the main road, but worth seeing, is Poughill (Puffle) church, dedicated to St Olaf, a Dane. There are two large wall representations of St Christopher, repainted by Frank Salisbury, and a Tazza Cup and Paten, beautifully shaped and richly decorated. The clock in the tower has a memorial tablet which is rarely seen; it says of Sir Goldsworthy Gurney: 'His inventions and discoveries in Steam and Electricity made communication by land and sea so rapid that it became necessary for all England to keep uniform clock time.'

Those following the coastal walk will have increasingly fine views, especially near Stowe Barton, where the road dips into the Coombe Valley. This handsome farm was built on the site of Sir Richard Grenville's home, unfortunately pulled down in 1739: today only the stables remain. Here one can obtain handknitted garments in silk, wool and cotton, while Cornish guernseys made to order are a speciality.

The bridge at Coombe carries a tablet — now very weathered — which commemorated King William IV's

Guildhall, Poundstock

contribution to its building. In the early days of the nineteenth century, when the ford here was a danger to the lives of men and animals, the Rev R.S. Hawker of Morwenstow appealed to the king for financial help, and eventually a bridge was built. Duckpool is a good place to swim, and the National Trust cliff Steeple Point affords an ideal vantage point for walkers. The nearby Coombe Valley is also Trust land. The cottage at the entrance to this valley is of special interest, though people rarely notice the cross-shaped window above the door. Here Hawker spent his honeymoon and began writing *Trelawney* — the poem which is now considered to be Cornwall's national anthem.

As the road climbs out of this valley, it continues north past the imposing sight of the dish aerials of the Government's

Places of Interest near Bude

Poundstock Church
Dedicated to the dwarf hermit, St Neot. Murals and exceptionally handsome bench ends are among the interesting features. Beside the churchyard is a Guildhall with a stormy history.

The Tree Inn
Stratton
Here Anthony Payne was born and died. Huge and faithful servant of Sir Bevil Grenville, especially at the battle of Stamford Hill.

Battle of Stamford Hill 1643
The site is near Stratton — in the field there is a commemorative plaque on the wall.

Kilkhampton

Composite Signals Organisation Station. Beyond is Morwenstow, almost the end of Cornwall, but full of history and known as Hawker country. For over forty years, till 1875, this famous parson-poet was vicar here. Wrongly styled an eccentric, he startled his fellow churchmen by righting many wrongs and frequently risking his life to rescue shipwrecked sailors and give Christian burial to the bodies of the drowned. In the churchyard is what might be considered a memorial to his brave dedication — the figurehead of the *Caledonia,* broken on the rocks below in 1842, leaving only one man alive. Petitioner for his parishioners' cause at a time of dire poverty and restorer of the Harvest Festival, Robert Stephen Hawker's achievements will long be remembered. He wrote fine poetry in a hut on the clifftop, now National Trust property, and his unique vicarage chimneys, modelled on church towers, can just be glimpsed in the woods below the church.

The Bush Inn, a few hundred yards away from the churchtown, is unusual in retaining the traditional sign once given to all taverns. It is an old inn, where the Morwenstow Union Friendly Society probably met in the late eighteenth century. It had a thatched roof until a few years ago, but now that has gone and some of its charm has disappeared.

The end of Cornwall is reached where Marsland Mouth lies below the Cliff — the scene of many shipwrecks in days of sail — but the lane turns inland to Woolley, where there is not an end but a

Places of Interest North of Bude

Hawker's Hut
Vicarage Cliff, Morwenstow
Perched on the edge of the cliff, overlooking the fearful rocks where so many ships foundered, and whose men he saved — Parson Hawker built his shelter. Access by footpath from churchyard gate.

Launcells Church
In a wooded valley beside St Swithin's Well, this is one of the gems of Cornwall. Encaustic tiles, box pews and a mediaeval mural.

beginning. Among the marshes at Woolley Barrows, Cornwall's river Tamar, which marks the boundary with Devon has its source. The A39 road south, once the pilgrim highway to St Michaels Mount, goes to Kilkhampton.

The church here is worth a visit because it has a splendid lych gate, good pew ends and Grenville memorials.

South of the village the blacksmith can be seen from a viewing window. He hammers out anything from a key rack to a boot valet for the Queen Mother — it is interesting to watch so safely.

From the B3254, the road leads to the Tamar lakes, with the usual reservoir pursuits. Both are beautiful and can be enjoyed by those who want only to picnic. Lower Lake was created in 1820 to feed the now obsolete Bude Canal.

Deep in the country is Launcells' unique church. Time has left it untouched, and a visit is a step back into history. Treasures like this — as with many in Cornwall — are not easily located but, when discovered, they are a source of delight for visitors who come to the Royal Duchy for a holiday that is different.

Further Information For Visitors

ACCOMMODATION

Cornwall offers a wide range of accommodation from luxury hotels to campsites. There are too many to include here but details can be obtained from the Cornwall Tourist Board or Information Centres.

ANNUAL EVENTS IN DATE ORDER

These are the best known of the wide variety of events which take place every year. The numerous carnivals, music festivals and regattas are widely advertised in local papers.

Towednack Cuckoo Feast: 28 April
Padstow 'Obby 'Oss: 1 May
Helston Flora Day: 8 May
Royal Cornwall Show, Wadebridge: second week in June
Old Cornwall Societies Bonfires: Midsummer eve
Stithians Show: second Monday in July
St Mellion Cherry Pie Feast: July
St Endellion Music and Drama Festival: end of July
Culdrose Air Day: end of July
Scilly Water Sports: beginning of August
RAF St Mawgan International Air Day: mid August
Oyster Boat Race. Falmouth to Fowey Harbour: end of Falmouth Regatta Week in August. Working Boats only.
Crying the Neck, Helston: last Friday in August
Cornish Gorsedd: first Saturday in September. Various venues.
(Eisteddfod 1983 and every 5 years.)
St Ives Festival: September

BOATING

Most resorts have boat trips: information about these and boats for hire is best found locally, usually near the pier or quay.

BUILDINGS OPEN TO THE PUBLIC

Details are correct at time of publication but they are subject to modification from year to year. Visitors are advised to check locally beforehand.

Antony House (NT)
2 miles NW of Torpoint, 16 miles SE of Liskeard, 15 miles E of Looe.
Tel: Plymouth 812191
Open: April-end of October, Tuesday, Wednesday, Thursday, Bank Holiday Monday 2-6pm. Closed Good Friday. (Last guided tour of house 5.30pm).

Cornish Mine Engines (NT)
On A3047 at Pool, near Camborne.
Open: April-end of October, daily (including Good Friday) 11am-6pm or sunset, if earlier. (Last admission half an hour before closing).

Cothele (NT)
2 miles E of St Dominick, 4 miles from Gunnislake (turn at St Anne's Chapel), 1 mile W of Calstock by footpath (6 miles by road).
Tel: St Dominick 50434
Open: April-end of October, daily 11am-6pm (Last admission 5-30pm). Shop and restaurant.

Egyptian House (NT)
Chapel Street, Penzance
Tel: Penzance 4378
Part of ground floor is NT Shop.
Open: weekdays 9am-5pm (Closed
January, February and March).

Godolphin House
Nr Helston (between villages of
Townshend and Godolphin Cross).
Tel: Germoe 2409
Open: May and June, Thursday 2-5pm;
July-September, Tuesday and Thursday
2-5pm.

Lanhydrock (NT)
$2\frac{1}{2}$ miles SE of Bodmin, follow signposts
from either A38 Bodmin-Liskeard or
B3268 Bodmin-Lostwithiel.
Tel: Bodmin 3320
Open: April-end of October, daily
including Bank Holidays and Good
Friday 11am-6pm (Last admission 5-
30pm).
Shop and refreshments.

**Mount Edgcumbe House and Country
Park**
Cremyll, near Saltash.
Open: House and higher gardens May-
30 September, Monday and Tuesday 2-
6pm. Park and lower garden all year,
free.
Refreshments in Orangery.

Pencarrow House
Washaway, Bodmin. 4 miles from
Bodmin, 3 miles from Wadebridge, near
junction of A389 and B3266.
Tel: St Mabyn 369
Open: House and Tearooms, Easter-end
of September daily, except Monday and
Saturday, 1.30-5pm (Bank Holiday
Mondays and 1 June-September 11am-
5pm). Guided tours. Self-pick soft fruit
when in season.

St Michael's Mount (NT)
$\frac{1}{2}$ mile S of Marazion (A394). Access on
foot at low tide, or by ferry.
Tel: Penzance 710507
Open: April-end of May, Monday,
Wednesday and Friday 10.30am-
5.45pm; from end October, Monday,
Tuesday, Wednesday and Friday
10.30am-5.45pm (Last admission
4.45pm).
Shop, refreshments, Island Cafe, April-
end September, Monday-Friday, during
opening hours.

Tintagel Old Post Office (NT)
Open: April-end of October, daily
11am-6pm (or sunset if earlier).
Shop.

Trecarrel Hall
Near Trebullet, $3\frac{1}{2}$ miles S of
Launceston, between A388 and B3254.
Tel: Mrs Burden, Coads Green 286 to
view.

Trelowarren
Mawgan-in-Meneage, near Helston.
From Helston take A3083 Lizard road,
then left on to B3293, signposted
Trelowarren.
Open: House open during August.
Home of the Vyvyan family.

Trerice (NT)
3 miles SE of Newquay via A392 and
A3058 (turn right at Kestle Mill).
Tel: Newquay 5404
Open: April-end of October, daily
11am-6pm (Last admission 5.30pm).
Shop and Restaurant.

Trewint, Wesley's Cottage
On A30 between Bodmin and
Launceston.
Methodist shrine in N Cornwall.
Open: daily. Admission free, collection
box.

CASTLES

All are historic monuments in the care of the Department of the Environment.

Launceston
Pendennis, Castle Drive, Falmouth
Restormel, Lostwithiel
St Catherine's, Fowey (free access)
St Mawes
Tintagel, Trevena

Carn Brea Castle, Redruth is an ancient monument now a licensed restaurant. Approach road from Carnkie Village. Reservations: Redruth 218358 Open: for lunches all year, except Mondays 12.30-2pm (Last orders Sundays 1pm). Teas daily, except Mondays 3-5pm July and August. Dinners daily all year, except Sunday and Monday 7-9.30pm.

CRAFT WORKSHOPS

The variety and range of craft workshops can only be indicated here. Smaller ones are to be found in unexpected, out of the way places.

Ironcraft

Calcraft Products
Wheal Arthur, Gunnislake
Signposted on Gunnislake to Tavistock road out of Calstock.
Tel: Tavistock 832648
Showroom and workshops open daily throughout the year 9am-6pm.
Reproduction arms and armour.

Cornish Ironcraft Co
Brentspool, Kilkhampton, Bude
On A39 S of Kilkhampton.
Tel: Kilhampton 350
Open: Monday-Saturday 10am-6pm, Sundays 12-5pm.
Viewing gallery to working forge. Shop.

Knitwear and Textiles

Madeline Hough
Stowe Barton, Kilkhampton, Nr Bude
On coast road north of Bude, 1 mile before Duckpool.
Tel: Morwenstow 233
Open: 10am-4pm. Display of hand knitwear in silk, wool and cotton. Cornish guernseys to order.

Leathercraft

St Eval Leather Crafts
Downhill, St Eval, Wadebridge
$\frac{3}{4}$ mile from St Eval Church SW 861690.
Tel: St Mawgan 357
Open: Monday-Friday 9am-4.30pm.
After 4.30pm by appointment only.
Hand made leather goods and reproductions of medieval leather vessels.

Pictures and Prints

Mullionaires Ltd
Nansmellyon Road, Mullion

Potteries

Fosters Pottery
Tolgus Hill, Redruth
Tel: Redruth 215754 and 213710
Open: Summer 9am-5pm weekdays, 10am-12 noon Saturdays.
Large showroom, guided tours, tearoom.

Kernewek Pottery
Goonhavern, Nr Perranporth
On A3070 Redruth to Newquay road.
Tel: Perranporth 3505
Open: June-September, weekdays 9am-9pm, Saturdays 9am-5pm, Sundays 10am-5pm.

Leach Pottery
Higher Stennack, St Ives
Tel: Penzance 796398
Showroom open in usual trading hours.

St Nectans Pottery
Nr St Nectans Glen, Trethewy, Tintagel
In farm courtyard on B3263 midway
between Tintagel and Boscastle.
Hand-thrown earthenware and
stoneware.
Workshop open daily 10am-dusk during
season.

Tremar Potteries
Penhale Grange, St Cleer, Liskeard
Tel: Liskeard 42771
Open: Showroom daily 10am-10pm, free
guided tours of workshops 10am-
4.30pm weekdays.

Trenquoit Pottery
Trethevy Quoit, Darite, Nr Liskeard
Tel: Liskeard 45978
Parking, showroom, admission free.

Truro Pottery and Kiln Museum
Chapel Hill, Truro
Oldest pottery in Cornwall.
Tel: Truro 2928
Shop and Museum open 9.30am-5pm,
Monday-Saturday all year except Bank
Holidays.
Cafeteria light refreshments.

Gardens

Glendurgan Garden (NT)
Helford River, 4 miles SW of Falmouth,
$\frac{1}{2}$ mile SW of Mawnan Smith on road to
Helford Passage.
Open: March-end October, Monday,
Wednesday and Friday (closed Good
Friday) 10.30am-4.30pm.

Ken-Caro
Bicton, Pensilva
Open: Wednesday and Sunday, May and
June 2-6pm.

Padstow Tropical Bird and Butterfly Gardens
Fentonluna Lane, Padstow
Tel: Padstow 532262
Open: Daily 10.30am-8pm summer, 5pm
winter.
Refreshment terrace open all summer.
Gift shop. Parking on link road B3276.

Penjerrick
Budock, Falmouth
3 miles from Falmouth on road to
Mawnan Smith.
Tel: Falmouth 250659
Open: Sunday and Wednesday 1.30-
4.30pm, March-end of September.
Gardens only, flowering in Spring with
rhododendrons, camellias, azaleas and
trees.

Trelissick Garden (NT)
4 miles S of Truro, on both sides of
B3289 above King Harry Ferry.
Tel: Truro 862090
Open: April-end October, Mondays-
Saturdays 11am-6pm or sunset if earlier,
Sunday 1-6pm.
Plants and souvenirs at garden shop.
Refreshments in barn.

Trengwainton Garden (NT)
2 miles NW of Penzance, $\frac{1}{2}$ mile W of
Heamoor on Penzance to Morvah road
(B3312) $\frac{1}{2}$ mile off St Just road (A3071).
Open: March-end October, Wednesday,
Thursday, Friday (including Good
Friday), Saturday and Bank Holiday
Monday 11am-6pm.

Tresco Abbey
Isles of Scilly
Tel: Scillonia 22849
Open: Monday-Saturday 10am-4pm.
Snack bar open in summer months.

Trewidden
Buryas Bridge, Penzance (Entrance off
Lands End Road A30).
Open regularly Monday-Friday and
March-end June, Saturdays 10am-5pm.

Trewithen Gardens

Grampound Road, Nr Truro (A390 between Probus and Grampound).
Open: 1 March - 30 September, Monday-Saturday 2-4.30pm. Nursery open all year round.
Free car parking, toilets (including disabled), garden shop, dogs on leads, picnics permitted.

GOLF CLUBS

Bude
Carlyon Bay, St Austell
Falmouth, Pennance
Isles of Scilly, St Mary's
Launceston, St Stephen
Looe Bin Down, Looe
Mullion
Newquay
Perranporth
St Austell
St Enodoc, Rock
St Mellion, Nr Saltash
Tehidy Park, Camborne
Trevose, Constantine Bay
Truro
West Cornwall, Lelant, Nr Hayle, St Ives
Whitesand Bay, St Germans

LIFEBOAT STATIONS

A number of these are open to the public depending on weather conditions.

Lifeboats
Coverack, Falmouth, Fowey, Lizard-Cadgwith, Newquay, Padstow, Penlee, Port Isaac, St Agnes, St Ives, St Mary's, Sennen Cove.

LIGHTHOUSES

An important feature of this sea-girt region, these masterpieces of engineering — some built locally — provide a circle of safety round the Western

Approaches. Four are open to the public:
Lizard
Pendeen, St Just
St Anthony, Roseland Peninsula
Trevose Head, Padstow

MAJOR ARCHAEOLOGICAL SITES

Cadsonbury
Near New Bridge, 2 miles SW of Callington (SX 345675)
An important univallate hill-fort at the crown of a steep lonely hill in the River Lynher valley. Not yet excavated, but probably of early Iron Age. There is footpath access from the New Bridge to Clapper Bridge road. (National Trust)

St Piran's Round
Perranporth (SW 779545)
This impressive Iron Age fortification, also called Piran or Perran Round, is an adaptation made in the Middle Ages for a *plain-an-gwarry* or open air theatre-in-the-round. High terraced banks round the huge amphitheatre serve for players and audience. Used successfully in 1969-73 for mediaeval drama revivals.

'The Hurlers' Stone Circles
$\frac{1}{2}$ mile NW of Minions (SX 255714)
Three large stone circles in a line, none of the monoliths exceeds 6ft in height. Early Bronze Age flints have been found here and the monument is considered one of the best of its type in the south-west. (Department of the Environment)

The Rumps
Pentire Point, north of the Camel Estuary (SW 935811)
One of the best examples of an Iron Age promontory fort. Three lines of defensive ramparts cut off the six-acre headland, one entrance serving the whole. Wheel-turned Iron Age pottery has been found here. (National Trust)

Trencrom Hill
3 miles S of St Ives (SW 518362)
Well-preserved Iron Age site of sixty-four acres, stone-walled and enclosing hut circles. Of legendary interest as the home of the Giant Trecobber who played bowls with his brother on St Michael's Mount. One of the bowls remains as Bowl Rock on the Lelant-Towednack road which runs below on the north side. (National Trust)

Treryn Dinas (Treen Cliff)
4 miles SE of Land's End (SW 398222)
Perhaps Cornwall's best-known cliff fort. The thirty-six acres include Logan Rock removed in 1824 by Lieutenant Goldsmith. The area has a five line complex of fortifications. (National Trust)

Trethevy Quoit
1 mile NE of St Cleer (SX 259688)
A closed megalithic burial chamber 7ft long and 9ft high. There are five standing stones supporting a huge capstone. (Department of the Environment)

Warbstow Bury
2 miles N of Hallworthy A396 (SX 201908)
A magnificent Celtic Iron Age fort with a double wall and two gateways, one of Cornwall's largest. Some claim that King Arthur lies in one of the graves of this great barrow.

Bants Carn Burial Chamber and Ancient Village
1 mile N of Hugh Town, St Mary's, Isles of Scilly (SV 911124)
A Bronze Age Burial chamber about 40ft diameter with entrance passage and outer and inner retaining walls. Nearby village huts were occupied in the mid-Roman period. (Department of the Environment)

MUSEUMS

This list excludes those buildings open to the public that have museums associated with them or other places that have special displays and are listed elsewhere.

Automobilia
The Old Mill, St Stephen, St Austell
4 miles off A30. Signposted from Summercourt on A3058.
Tel: St Austell 823092
Open: Daily 10am-7pm.
Motor museum, historic photographs, gift and model shop. Cafe. Free parking.

Barbara Hepworth Museum and Sculpture Garden
Trewyn Studio and Garden, Barnoon Hill, St Ives
Tel: Penzance 796226
Open: July and August 10am-6.30pm, Sundays 2-6pm. April-June, September 10am-5.30pm. Closed Sundays. October-March 10am-4.30pm. Closed Sundays.
Administered by the Tate Gallery.

Barnes Cinematograph Museum
Fore Street, St Ives
Open: Daily 11am-1pm, 2.30-5pm.

Bude Historical and Folk Exhibition
The Old Forge, Town Wharf, Bude
Tel: Bude 3576
Open: Monday-Friday 9am-5pm.
Maintained by Bude-Stratton Town Council.

Camborne Museum
Public Library, The Cross, Camborne
Open: 3-5pm weekdays (except Thursday), 10am-12 noon Saturdays.
Admission free.
Mining exhibits and photographs, early coins and many other local items.

Camborne School of Mines Museum
On A3047 midway between Camborne and Redruth.
Open all year Monday-Friday, excluding Bank Holidays 9am-4.30pm.
Admission free.

Cornish Folk Museum
East Looe
Open: May - September, Monday -
Friday 11am-5pm.

Dairyland
Tresillian Barton, Summercourt,
Newquay
On A3058 Newquay to Summercourt
road.
Tel: Mitchell 246
Open: Daily 22 March - 5 November,
1.30-5pm. Easter week and May -
October 10am-5pm. Milking 3.15-
4.30pm.
Working farm with one of Europe's
most modern parlours and country life
museum. Facilities for disabled. Picnic
area, farmyard and playground. Free
parking.

Delabole Slate Museum
Pengelly House, Delabole
B3314 to Delabole then follow AA signs.
Tel: Camelford 212242
Open: Monday - Friday 10am-5pm,
April - September.
Museum and gift shop.

The Duke of Cornwall's Light Infantry
Regimental Museum
The Keep, Bodmin
Tel: Bodmin 2810
$\frac{1}{4}$ mile south of town centre on B3269
Open: Monday - Friday 9.30am-
12.30pm, 2-4.30pm. Closed on Bank
Holidays. Parties at other times by
arrangement.

Falmouth Maritime Museum
Steam tug *St Denys,* Custom House
Quay, Falmouth
Open: Daily 10am to sunset.

Fowey Town Museum
Trafalgar Square, Fowey
Open: Monday - Saturday 10.30am-12
noon, 2.30-4.30pm April - September.
Local History.

Geevor Tin Mines
Pendeen,Penzance
On B3306, St Just to St Ives road at
Pendeen.
Tel: Office - Penzance 788662
      Shop & Museum - Penzance 788030
Open: Daily April - October 10am-
5.30pm.
Unique Cornish mining museum, gift
and souvenir shop, refreshments.
Guided tours of working treatment plant
producing tin concentrate Monday -
Friday 10.30am-4pm except Bank
Holidays. School parties welcomed by
prior arrangement.

Guildhall Museum
Fore Street, Lostwithiel
Tel: Bodmin 872380
Open: Easter week, then mid-May - 30
September.
Historical guided tour for parties.
Museum free.

Helston Folk Museum
The Old Butter Market, Helston
Open: Monday - Saturday 10.30am-
12.30pm, 2-4.30pm (closed Wednesday
12 noon).

Isles of Scilly Museum
Church Street, St Mary's
Tel: Scillonia 22337 or 22691 (Hon Sec)
Open: Daily except Sundays April -
October 10am-12 noon, 1.30-4.30pm.
    also Whitsun - September 7.30-9pm.
    Winter Wednesday 2-4pm.

Lanreath Mill and Farm Museum
Churchtown, Lanreath, Looe
$\frac{1}{2}$ mile off B3359 midway between
Taphouse and Looe.
Tel: Lanreath 20321 or 20349
Open: Easter - October 10am-1pm, 2-
6pm.
Craft demonstrations most afternoons.

Lawrence House (NT)
Castle Street, Launceston
Open: April-end September, Monday-
Friday (closed Good Friday) 10.30am-
12.30pm, 2.30-4.30pm.
Tel: Launceston 2833
Admission free, but contributions
invited.

Looe Aquarium
The Quay, East Looe
Open: Daily 10am-9pm.

Pendeen Crafts and Mining Museum
Boscaswell
Open: normal shopping hours during
the season.

Penryn Local History Museum
Town Hall, Penryn
Open: Monday-Friday 9am-12.30pm, 2-
5pm.

**Royal Institution of Cornwall Museum
and Art Gallery**
River Street, Truro
Tel: Truro 2205
Open: Weekdays 9am-1pm, 2-5pm.
October-March closed on Mondays.

St Ives Museum
Wheal Dream, St Ives
Behind Smeaton's Pier.
Open: Monday-Friday 10.30am-5pm
during summer.
Maritime History.

Shire Horse Farm and Carriage Museum
Lower Grylls Farm, Treskillard,
Redruth
Leave Camborne by-pass at Pool
turning, A3047, across traffic lights, turn
right over railway bridge, follow
signposts to Carriage Museum.
Tel: Camborne 713606
Open: Daily 10am-6pm Easter-
September.
Free wagon rides at 11am and 4pm-
Picnic area, farm walk, farmhouse
cream teas.

Tolgus Tin
New Portreath Road, Redruth
Between Redruth and Portreath on
B3300.
Tel: Redruth 215171
Open: Daily 10am-6pm, 26 April-30
September (last tour 5.15pm). Guided
tour through old Cornish tin mill (all
under cover).
Exhibition and audio visual
presentation, children's amusements,
cafe, free car park, picnic area, mineral
and gift shop.

Wayside Museum
Zennor, St Ives
On B3306 Lands End to St Ives road at
Zennor.
Open: 9.30am to dusk daily May-
October.
Mining, fishing, quarrying, agricultural
and craft implements, domestic utensils,
old mill and open hearth. Admission
free.

Wheal Martyn China Clay Museum
Carthew, St Austell
Follow signposts to Carthew on A391 2
miles N of St Austell.
Tel: St Austell 850362
Open: Daily April-end October 10am-
6pm (last admission 5pm).
Complete nineteenth-century clay
works. Working waterwheels, wagons,
locomotives, craft pottery and
introductory slide programme.

NATURE TRAILS

Most nature trails in Cornwall and the
Isles of Scilly are laid out by the Forestry
Commission, the National Trust or the
South West Water Authority.

Cardinham Woods
Off A38 Bodmin to Plymouth Road, 2
miles E of Bodmin. SX 099664. Forestry
Commission leaflet available.

Coombe Valley
On coast road 3 miles W of
Kilkhampton and 5 miles N of Bude. SS
213117. Two trails laid out by National
Trust. Booklet from local bookshops.

Coulson Park
Lostwithiel

Deerpark Forest
Off Taphouse to Looe road B3359 near
Herodsfoot. SX 197603. Forestry
Commission leaflet available.

Duchy Nurseries
Lostwithiel

Halvana Forest Trail
Off A30 from Five Lanes. SX 213788.
Leaflet available.

Trelissick (National Trust)

Lanhydrock (National Trust)

St Clement Wood
Near Idless, 2 miles N of Truro.
SW 819479.

St Mary's
Isles of Scilly
Two nature trails at Holy Vale and the
Moors.

RESERVOIR RECREATION

Reservoirs provide a wide range of
opportunities for enjoyment. Most are
open for fishing; on some it is possible to
sail, canoe or even water ski. Many are
superb places for a picnic, and to sit and
watch the ever-changing scene of water,
boats, fishermen and birds, or to stroll
through some of Cornwall's most
beautiful scenery.
Not all the reservoirs are open for every
facility, but each year sees a broadening
of those available. In this way it is hoped
to increase the areas of peace and quiet
for pure enjoyment of the countryside.

For information regarding permits
apply to:
Information Office,
Fisheries and Recreation,
South West Water Authority,
3-5 Barnfield Road,
Exeter, Devon.
Tel: Exeter 31666

Argal-College
Off B3281 Penryn to Constantine road.
Birdwatching, stocked trout fishing (fly
only), coarse fishing, picnicking, toilets
and walking.

Colliford
Under construction.

Crowdy
Off A39 Camelford to Bude road.
General access, birdwatching and
natural trout fishing.

Porth
Off A3059 Newquay to Wadebridge
road.
Birdwatching, and stocked trout fishing
(fly only).

Siblyback
Between A30 Bodmin to Launceston
road and A38 Bodmin to Liskeard road.
Picnicking, walking, toilets, play area,
refreshments kiosk, birdwatching,
sailing, boardsailing, canoeing, water
skiing and stocked trout fishing (fly
only).

Stithians
Between A394 Falmouth to Helston and
A393 Falmouth to Redruth roads.
Birdwatching, sailing and boardsailing,
canoeing, rowing, water skiing and
natural trout fishing (fly only).

Tamar Lakes
Off A39 at Kilkhampton.
Picnicking, walking, toilets,
birdwatching refreshment kiosk, sailing,
boardsailing, canoeing, stocked trout
fishing (fly only) and mixed trout and
coarse fishing.

RIDING AND PONY TREKKING

The following are some of the licensed riding establishments offering riding and trekking holidays.

Tall Trees Riding Stables, Davidstow, Camelford
Mr B.R.J. Young, Ninestones Farm, St Cleer, Liskeard
Miss G.E.S. Alexander, Woodlands, St Blazey
Old Mill Stables, Lelant Downs
Rosehill Riding School, Rosehill, Penzance

SPORTS AND LEISURE CENTRES

Carn Brea Leisure Centre
Station Road, Pool, Redruth
Just off the A3047 Camborne-Redruth road at mini-roundabout.
Tel: Camborne 714766
Open: 9am-10.30pm daily.
Largest leisure centre in Cornwall. coaching courses in various sporting activities. Parking space for 400 cars.

Climbers Club
The Count House, Bosigran, Pendeen, St Ives

Cornish Gliding & Flying Club
Perranporth Airfield

Cornish Leisure World
Carlyon Bay, St Austell

Cornwall Flying Club
Bodmin Airfield, Cardinham

Polkyth Recreation Centre
Carlyon Road, St Austell

STEAM AND OTHER RAILWAYS

Forest Railroad Park
½ mile N of A38 at Dobwalls (between Liskeard and Bodmin).
Tel: Dobwalls 20325
Open: Daily Easter-end September 10am-5.30pm.
Cafe, picnic areas, toilets, car park. A theme park based on the American Railways in miniature. Film shows, model lay-outs, loco sheds, hall of memories, etc.

Gwinear Outdoor Model Railway
Off A30 Camborne to Hayle road. Look for Blue Tourist Information caravan on A30 and turn off for Carnhill Green.
Tel: Praze 831537
Open: Easter-September 10am till dusk all weathers.
3,000ft track of 00-gauge railway. 'U.Drive' Scalextric layout. Model shop. Cafe.

Lappa Valley Railway and Leisure Park
Newlyn East, Newquay
5 miles from Newquay. Follow signs to Newlyn East then special signs to railway.
Tel: Mitchell 317
Open: 1.30-6pm during season.
Car park, buffet, licensed restaurant, old engine house and chimney stack of disused East Wheal Rose mine. 2 mile round trip in roomy carriages.

Mevagissey Model Railway
Meadow Street, Mevagissey
Tel: Mevagissey 842457
Open: Summer 11am-5pm (9pm during high season)
Winter, Sundays only 2-5pm.
One of world's unique collections of model railways (nearly 1,500 items) and large working layout. Suitable for wheelchairs.

TOURIST INFORMATION CENTRES

These are run by local authorities with the assistance of the Cornwall Tourist Board.

Cornwall Tourist Board HQ
County Hall grounds, Station Road, Truro
Tel: Truro (0872) 74288
Open all year Monday - Friday 9am-5pm.

A39 Bude
Stamford Hill, Stratton
Tel: Bude (0288) 3781
Open from Spring Bank Holiday until late September.

A30 Connor Downs
Near Hayle and serving Penzance, St Ives and the Land's End Penninsula
Tel: Camborne (0209) 714742

A394 Helston
Greenacres, Clodgey Lane
Tel: Helston (03265) 62505

A39 Perranarworthal
Near Falmouth and also serving The Lizard area
Tel: Truro (0872) 863946

A30 Roche
Near Newquay with St Austell bay to the south
Tel: Roche (0726) 890481

A38 Tideford
Heskyn Hill, soon after entering Cornwall from Plymouth
Tel: Landrake (07538) 397

TRANSPORT

Ferries C=Car, F=Foot
Plymouth (Devonport) to Torpoint (C)
Plymouth (Stonehouse) to Cremyll (F)
Fowey to Polruan (F)
Fowey to Bodinnick (C)
Padstow to Rock (F)
Falmouth to St Mawes (F)
Falmouth to Flushing (F)
Feock to Philleigh (King Harry) (C)
Penzance to Isles of Scilly (St Mary's)
Inter-island launch services leave for the offshore islands shortly after arrival of the ship at St Mary's. Boatmen's Association launches leave daily at 10.15am and 2.15pm during summer.

Isles of Scilly Steamship Co Ltd,
Quay Street,
Penzance TR18 4BD
Tel: Penzance 2009 or 4013

British Airways Helicopters,
Heliport
Penzance
Tel: Penzance 3871

Western National Bus Co,
Bus Station,
Lemon Quay,
Truro
Tel: Truro 3157

Brymon Airways,
Newquay Civil Airport
Tel: St Mawgan 551

British Rail. For all passenger train and fares enquiries telephone Truro 76244 (7.30am-10pm daily).

USEFUL ADDRESSES

'Adventure Days' (Surfing, Enquiries and Bookings),
7 Belle Vue,
Bude, Cornwall

British Horse Society,
Kenilworth,
Warwickshire CV8 2LR
(Pony Trekking and Riding Holidays)

British Tourist Authority,
Information Centre,
64 St James' Street,
London SW1
Tel: 01 499 9325

Camping Club of Great Britain and
Ireland,
11 Lower Grosvenor Place,
London SW1W 0EY
Tel: 01 828 1012

Canoeing Courses (Enquiries and
Bookings),
Forge Cottage,
Clubworthy,
North Petherwin PL15 8NZ

Caravan Club,
East Grinstead House,
East Grinstead,
Sussex RH19 1UA
Tel: 0342 26944

Cornwall Birdwatching and Preservation
Society,
Treasurer and Registrar: Mr W.K.J. Grey,
12 Chynance Drive,
Newquay
Tel: 06373 5604

Council for the Protection of Rural
England,
4 Hobart Place,
London SW1W 0HY
Tel: 01 235 9481

Cyclists Touring Club,
69 Meadrow,
Godalming,
Surrey GU7 3HS
Tel: Godalming 7217

Department of the Environment,
(Ancient Monuments Commission),
25 Savile Row,
London W1X 2BT
Tel: 01 734 6010

Forestry Commission,
Kernow Forest Office,
Ashgrove,
Dunmere,
Bodmin PL31 2DU
Tel: Bodmin 2577

Holiday Fellowship,
142 Great North Way,
London NW4 1EG
Tel: 01 203 3381

Isles of Scilly Information Office,
Town Hall,
St Mary's
Isles of Scilly TR21 0LW
Tel: Scillonia 22536

National Trust,
42 Queen Anne's Gate,
London SW1H 9AS
Tel: 01 222 9251

National Trust,
Cornwall Information Office,
The Estate Office,
Lanhydrock Park,
Bodmin,
Cornwall PL30 4DE
Tel: Bodmin 4281

Ramblers Association,
1-5 Wandsworth Road,
London SW8 2LJ
Tel: 01 582 6878
Area Secretary: Alfred Palmer,
1 Whitley Barn,
Tresarrett,
Bodmin PL30 4QH
Tel: Bodmin 850831

South West Arts,
23 Southernhay East,
Exeter EX1 1QG
Tel: 0392 38924

VISITOR CENTRES

Aero Park and Flambards Village
Helston side of Culdrose Air Station, off the main A3083 Lizard road.
Tel: Helston 4549 or 3404
Open: Daily Easter-November 10am-5pm

Bird Paradise and Children's Zoo
$\frac{1}{4}$ mile on B3302 from A30 at Hayle.
Tel: Hayle 753365
Open: 10am to dusk all year round.

Bodmin Farm Park
Fletchers Bridge, Bodmin
Off A38 Bodmin-Liskeard road at Fletchers Bridge signpost.
Tel: Bodmin 2074
Open: Mid-May-September, daily (except Saturday) 10am-6pm. Last admission 5pm.
Nature trail, children's activities, refreshments and gift shop.

Charlestown Visitor Centre
Charlestown, St Austell
Open: Daily from mid-April-mid-October 10am-6pm (open till dusk high season).
Eighteenth-century harbour village and shipwreck centre.

Lelant Model Park
Lelant, St Ives
Off A30 near Hayle on A3074 to St Ives.
Tel: Hayle 752676
Open: Daily Easter-end October 10am-5pm (High season 10am-10pm).
Toilets, free car park. Attractions include junior commando course.

Newquay Zoo and Leisure Park
5 minutes from town centre on the Edgecumbe Road/Trevemper Road.
Tel: Newquay 3342
Open: Daily from 10am.
Cafe.

Penwith Pleasure Park
Rospeath, Crowlas, Penzance
Off A30 at Crowlas.
Tel: Cockwells 740621
Open: Daily April-October 10am-1 hour after sunset.

Poldark Mine
Wendron
3 miles N of Helston on B3297 (Redruth road).
Tel: Helston 3531 or 3173
Open: Daily 10am-6pm (last tour of mine starts 5.15pm) April-October inclusive.
Tin mine, museums, historic engines, restaurant, shop, children's play area.
Not suitable for disabled people.

St Agnes Model Village
Tel: St Agnes 2793
Open: mid-March-September 9am-5pm.

YACHTING AND SAILING CLUBS

Cargreen,
F.N. Hele,
4 Coombe Lane,
Cargreen

Falmouth Docks,
J. Treen,
6 Frobisher Terrace,
Falmouth

Flushing,
New Quay,
Flushing

Fowey Gallants,
Mrs P. Sheridan,
Amity Court,
Fowey

Helford River,
D.L.W. Hale,
Flushing Cove,
Helston

Looe,
A. Garden,
Buller Street,
Looe

Mounts Bay,
(Hon Treasurer) P.F. Hoskins,
Godolphin Steps,
Marazion

Mylor,
T.J. Page,
Mylor Harbour,
Falmouth

Newquay,
W.T. Cole,
Towan House,
Gaverigan,
St Columb

Padstow,
R.J. Simpson,
School House,
Molesworth Street,
Wadebridge

Pentewan Sands,
(Hon Treasurer) G.E. Mitchell,
Greystones,
London Apprentice,
St Austell

Penzance,
J.M. Lees,
Albert Pier,
Penzance

Percuil,
Mrs J.W. Webb,
Westward,
Percuil, Portscatho

Porthpean,
Miss D.M. Berry,
37 Dennison Avenue,
St Austell

Royal Cornwall,
Mrs M. Muirhead,
Greenbank,
Falmouth

Royal Fowey,
T.K. Jones,
Whitford Yard,
Fowey

St Ives,
J.M. Cutler,
22 Bedford Road,
St Ives

St Mawes,
R.F. Wylie,
Lantreath,
St Mawes

Saltash,
Clubhouse,
Waterside,
Saltash

Scillonian,
C/o Harbour Master,
St Mary's

YOUTH HOSTELS

Youth Hostels Association,
Trevelyan House,
St Albans,
Herts AL1 2DY
Tel: St Albans 55215

Hostels at:
Boscastle, Palace Stabs
Coverack, Parc Behan
Falmouth, Pendennis Castle
Fowey, Penquite House, Golant
Hayle, Riviere House, Phillack
Mevagissey, Boswinger, Gorran
Newquay, Alexandra Court,
    Narrowcliffe
Padstow, Tregonnan, Treyarnon Bay
Penzance, Castle Horneck, Alverton
Perranporth, Droskyn Point
St Just in Penwith, Letcha Vean
Tintagel, Dunderhole Point

Index

BOOKS FROM MOORLAND WITH LOCAL INTEREST

Buildings of Britain:
SOUTH WEST ENGLAND £8.95

Archaeological Sites of
Devon and Cornwall
(£7.50 hardback & £4.95 paperback)

A Guide to
Stationary Steam Engines £4.95pb.

Mining in Cornwall
(2 volumes £3.50 each)